VALUATION WORKBOOK

The Wiley Finance series contains books written specifically for finance and investment professionals as well as sophisticated individual investors and their financial advisors. Book topics range from portfolio management to e-commerce, risk management, financial engineering, valuation and financial instrument analysis, as well as much more. For a list of available titles, visit our Web site at www.WileyFinance.com.

Founded in 1807, John Wiley & Sons is the oldest independent publishing company in the United States. With offices in North America, Europe, Australia and Asia, Wiley is globally committed to developing and marketing print and electronic products and services for our customers' professional and personal knowledge and understanding.

VALUATION WORKBOOK

SIXTH EDITION

McKinsey & Company

Tim Koller
Marc Goedhart
David Wessels
Michael Cichello

WILEY

Cover image: ©iStock.com/alzajac
Cover design: Wiley

Published by John Wiley & Sons, Inc., Hoboken, New Jersey.
Published simultaneously in Canada.

Cloth edition: ISBN 978-1-118-87370-0

Cloth edition with DCF Model Download: ISBN 978-1-118-87368-7

University edition: ISBN 978-1-118-87373-1

Workbook: ISBN 978-1-118-87387-8

DCF Model Download: ISBN 978-1-118-87366-3

Printed in the United States of America

10 9 8 7 6 5 4 3 2 1

Contents

About the Authors

The authors, collectively, have more than 50 years of experience in consulting and financial education.

Tim Koller is a partner in McKinsey's New York office, where he leads a global team of corporate-finance expert consultants. In his 30 years in consulting, Tim has served clients globally on corporate strategy and capital markets, mergers and acquisitions (M&A) transactions, and value-based management. He leads the firm's research activities in valuation and capital markets. Before joining McKinsey, he worked with Stern Stewart & Company and with Mobil Corporation. He received his MBA from the University of Chicago.

Marc Goedhart is a senior expert in McKinsey's Amsterdam office and leads the firm's Corporate Performance Center in Europe. Over the past 20 years, Marc has served clients across Europe on portfolio restructuring, capital markets, and M&A transactions. He taught finance as an assistant professor at Erasmus University in Rotterdam, where he also earned a PhD in finance.

David Wessels is an adjunct professor of finance at the Wharton School of the University of Pennsylvania. Named by *Bloomberg BusinessWeek* as one of America's top business school instructors, he teaches courses on corporate valuation and private equity at the MBA and executive MBA levels. David is also a director in Wharton's executive education group, serving on the executive development faculties of several Fortune 500 companies. A former consultant with McKinsey, he received his PhD from the University of California at Los Angeles.

Michael Cichello is a faculty member at the McDonough School of Business at Georgetown University. He teaches corporate valuation to undergraduate and masters students and works with executives to implement value creating opportunities. His research explores managerial incentives, corporate governance and financial contracting schemes. Professor Cichello received a PhD in finance from Michigan State University.

McKinsey & Company is a global management-consulting firm that serves leading businesses, governments, nongovernmental organizations, and not-for-profits across a wide range of industries and functions, helping them make distinctive, lasting, and substantial improvements in performance and realize their most important goals. McKinsey consultants serve clients in every region from a network of over 100 offices in more than 60 countries, advising on topics including strategy, finance, operations, organization, technology, marketing and sales, risk, and sustainability and resource productivity.

Introduction

The purpose of any workbook is to actively engage the reader/learner in the transfer of knowledge from author to reader. Although there are many levels at which knowledge can be transferred, the *Valuation Workbook* endeavors to provide the following three services:

1. A walk-through accompaniment to *Valuation: Measuring and Managing the Value of Companies,* Sixth Edition.
2. A summary of each chapter.
3. Tests of comprehension and skills of many types.

Multiple-choice questions pique your memory as you read the text. Lists and table completions force you to actively rearrange concepts, explicitly or implicitly, within the text. Calculation questions allow you to apply the skills deployed by the authors in accomplishing the analysis called valuation.

Our aim is to encourage you to question what you read against the background of your own business experience and to think about new ways to analyze and approach valuation issues.

VALUATION WORKBOOK

Part One

Questions

1

Why Value Value?

The chief measures for judging a company are its ability to create value for its shareholders and the amount of total value it creates. Corporations that create value in the long term tend to increase the welfare of shareholders and employees as well as improve customer satisfaction; furthermore, they tend to behave more responsibly as corporate entities. Ignoring the importance of value creation not only hurts the company but leads to detrimental results such as market bubbles.

Value creation occurs when a company generates cash flows at rates of return that exceed the cost of capital. Accomplishing this goal usually requires that the company have a competitive advantage. Activities such as leverage and accounting changes do not create value. Frequently, managers shortsightedly emphasize earnings per share (EPS); in fact, a poll of managers found that most managers would reduce discretionary value-creating activities such as research and development (R&D) in order to meet short-term earnings targets. One method to meet earnings targets is to cut costs, which may have short-term benefits but can have long-run detrimental effects.

1. Data from both Europe and the United States found that companies that created the most shareholder value showed ____________ employment growth.
2. In the past 30 years there have been at least ____________ financial crises that arose largely because companies and banks were ____________.
3. Two activities that managers often use in an attempt to increase share price but that do not actually create value are changes in ____________ and changes in ____________________.
4. Maximizing current share price is not equivalent to maximizing long-term value because ____________________.

5. During the Internet boom of the late 1990s, many firms lost sight of value creation principles by blindly pursuing ______________ without ______________.

6. The empirical evidence shows that the link between the value created by the acquisition of another company and earnings per share (EPS):
   A. Is strong and positive.
   B. Does not exist.
   C. Is weak and negative.
   D. Is strong and negative.

7. Paying attention to which of the following tends to lead to a company doing well in the stock market?
   I. Cash flow.
   II. Earnings per share.
   III. Growth.
   IV. Return on invested capital.
   A. I and II only.
   B. II and III only.
   C. II, III, and IV only.
   D. I, III, and IV only.

8. A firm that grows rapidly will:
   A. Always create value.
   B. Create value if the return on invested capital (ROIC) is greater than the cost of obtaining funds.
   C. Create value if the return on invested capital (ROIC) is less than the cost of obtaining funds.
   D. Create value if the firm increases market share.

9. In order to create long-term value, companies must:
   A. Focus on keeping costs at a minimum.
   B. Find the optimal debt-to-equity ratio.
   C. Seek and exploit new sources of competitive advantage.
   D. Monitor and follow macroeconomic trends.

10. The recent experience with the securitization of risky home loans illustrated how:
   A. Value could be created by the diversification of risk and increased number of investors.
   B. Value could be created by the diversification of risk only.
   C. Value could be created by the increased number of investors only.
   D. Value cannot be created by securitization.

2

Fundamental Principles of Value Creation

Earnings generation and value creation are correlated over the long run, but they are not the same. Value creation is determined by cash flows, which can be disaggregated into revenue growth and return on invested capital (ROIC). For any level of growth, increasing ROIC increases value; however, the reverse is not true. When ROIC is greater than the cost of capital, increasing growth increases the value of the firm; when ROIC is less than the cost of capital, increasing growth decreases the firm's value. When ROIC equals the cost of capital, growth does not affect a firm's value.

For the years 1995 to 2013, Rockwell Automation provides a good example of the importance of increasing ROIC. Over the period, revenue shrank by 4 percent per year, but ROIC increased from 12 percent to 32 percent.

The key value driver formula, is:

$$\text{Value} = \frac{\text{NOPLAT}_{t=1} \cdot \left(1 - \frac{\text{growth}}{\text{ROIC}}\right)}{\text{WACC} - \text{growth}}$$

where NOPLAT is the net operating profit less adjusted taxes.

Because the formula assumes the relationships are static, it may not be very useful in practice; however, it does outline the important relationships that determine and drive value. Part Two of the text expands on the formula.

1. Rank the types of growth from highest to lowest, where highest = 1, in terms of the amount of shareholder value each typically creates from the same incremental increase in revenue.

Types of growth	Ranking
A. Increase share in a growing market.	1.
B. Expand an existing market.	2.
C. Acquire businesses.	3.
D. Introduce new products to market.	4.

2. High-ROIC companies typically create more value by ____________, while lower-ROIC companies create more value by ____________.
3. Most often in mature companies, a low ROIC indicates ____________ ____________.
4. Complete the following sentence concerning the relationships among earnings, cash flow, and value. Earnings and cash flow are often ____________, but earnings don't tell the whole story of value creation, and focusing too much on earnings or earnings growth ____________.
5. When ROIC is greater than the cost of capital, the relationship between growth and value is ____________. When ROIC is less than the cost of capital, the relationship between growth and value is ____________. When ROIC equals the cost of capital, the relationship between growth and value is ____________.
6. With respect to countries, the core valuation principle is ____________, as made evident by the fact that U.S. companies trade ____________ companies in other countries.
7. When comparing the effect of an increase in growth on a high-ROIC company and a low-ROIC company, a 1 percent increase in growth will have ____________.
8. At high levels of ROIC, improving ROIC by increasing margins will create ____________ value than an equivalent ROIC increase by improving capital productivity.
9. Economic profit is the spread between ____________ and ____________ times ____________.
10. If the growth of a company is 2 percent and the ROIC is 10 percent, what is the investment rate?

    A. 2 percent.

    B. 5 percent.

    C. 12 percent.

    D. 20 percent.

11. For a given company, next year's NOPLAT is $300. For the foreseeable future, the growth rate will be 5 percent, the ROIC will be 15 percent, and the weighted average cost of capital (WACC) will be 13 percent. Using the key driver formula, calculate the value of the company.

    A. $1,666.

    B. $2,222.

    C. $2,500.

    D. $2,750.

3

Conservation of Value and the Role of Risk

In Chapter 2, we showed how cash flow drives value creation, and how growth and ROIC generate cash flow. Companies create value when they grow at returns on capital greater than their cost of capital or when they increase their returns on capital. The corollary, called the conservation of value, is that actions that don't increase cash flows over the long term will not create value, regardless of whether they improve earnings or otherwise make financial statements look stronger. One exception could be actions that reduce a company's risk and, therefore, its cost of capital.[1] As risk is not well understood in corporate finance, this chapter also explores different types of risk and how they enter into a company's valuation.

1. Changing capital structure creates value only if it ______________________________.
2. An acquisition will create value only if it increases cash flows by ______________________________.
3. For publicly traded companies, nondiversifiable risk affects the ______________________________, and diversifiable risk ______________________________.
4. Diversifiable risk arises from ______________________________.
5. Managers should hedge only risks that are ______________________________.
6. Managers should not take on cash flow risk that ______________________________.

[1]Technically, only risk reductions that reduce a company's nondiversifiable risk will reduce its cost of capital, as this chapter explains later.

7. When the likelihood of investing cash at ____________ is ____________, share repurchases make sense as a tactic for avoiding value destruction.
8. With respect to value creation, define financial engineering.
9. Because interest expense is tax deductible, share repurchases can have the beneficial effect of ________________________, but this may not increase share price because ________________________.
10. Studies of share repurchases have shown that companies ____________ at timing share repurchases, often ____________.

4

The Alchemy of Stock Market Performance

The expectations treadmill is the name for a problem faced by high-performing managers who try to meet the high market expectations that result from the high level of performance in recent periods. It's the reason that, in the short term, extraordinary managers may deliver only mediocre total returns to shareholders (TRS). It's also the dynamic behind the adage that a good company and a good investment may not be the same. An example of this is a comparison of the company and stock performance of Reckitt Benckiser Group (RB) and Henkel from 2008 to 2013. Although RB outperformed Henkel in both revenue growth and ROIC, the annualized TRSs were 19 and 32 percent, respectively. This may be because Henkel's low starting multiple in 2008 reflected difficulties with its adhesives business, which experienced significant declines in sales volume in 2008 and 2009.

Decomposing TRS can give better insights into a company's true performance and in setting new targets. There is already the traditional method of decomposing TRS into three parts: (1) percent change in earnings, (2) percent change in P/E, and (3) dividend yield. A clearer picture can be found from breaking TRS into four parts: (1) the value generated from revenue growth net of the capital required to grow, (2) the growth in TRS that would have taken place without the measure in (1), (3) changes in shareholder's expectations about the company's performance as reflected in a measure such as P/E, and (4) the effect of leverage. A more thorough analysis can explain why a small decline in TRS in the short run to adjust expectations may be preferable to desperately trying to maintain TRS through acquisitions and ill-advised ventures.

Use the following financials to answer Questions 1 through 4.

$ million	Base year	1 year later
Invested capital	$200	$206.6
Earnings	$20	$22
P/E	12	12.6
Equity value	240	277.2
Dividends	$10	$12

1. What is the TRS from performance?
   A. –2.0 percent.
   B. –0.5 percent.
   C. 4.5 percent.
   D. 6.7 percent.
2. What is the dividend yield?
   A. 4.2 percent.
   B. 4.8 percent.
   C. 5.0 percent.
   D. 6.0 percent.
3. What is the zero-growth return?
   A. 8.3 percent.
   B. 10.5 percent.
   C. 12.5 percent.
   D. 15.3 percent.
4. What is the TRS?
   A. 14.0 percent.
   B. 15.0 percent.
   C. 15.5 percent.
   D. 20.0 percent.
5. Using the traditional approach, an analyst can break down TRS into two or three components.
   List the components in the two-component breakdown:
   A. ____.
   B. ____.

   List the components in the three-component breakdown:
   A. ____.
   B. ____.
   C. ____.

6. For periods of ____________ years or more, it is true that if managers focus on ____________, then their interests and the interests of shareholders should be aligned.
7. The detrimental result of the expectations treadmill is that, for firms that have had superior operating and TRS performance, the managers who try to continually meet the higher expectations may engage in detrimental activities such as ____________ or ____________.
8. A company should measure management performance in terms of the company's performance, not its share price. Three areas of focus should be ____________, ____________, and ____________.

5

The Stock Market Is Smarter Than You Think

Return on invested capital (ROIC) and growth are the only drivers of value creation, yet managers often spend time and resources attempting to smooth earnings, meet earnings targets, stay listed in a stock index, and become cross-listed. The evidence shows that the stock market does not reward these efforts, nor do changes in accounting rules and stock splits have lasting effects. These issues do not have an effect on stock returns unless they reflect a change in fundamental value.

Listing and delisting from an index do not seem to have long-term effects for any given firm. Although there can be a negative effect initially from delisting, the effect usually reverses in a few months. Furthermore, cross-listing within developed markets does not have an effect; however, firms in emerging markets may benefit from cross-listing in a developed market.

Investors apparently see through accounting changes. If investors focused on earnings, for example, a move from FIFO to LIFO would lower the share price, but it generally does the opposite because of the increase in cash flows. As another example, mere changes in goodwill do not affect share price; however, a change in goodwill that is associated with a real change in the firm produces a reaction from sophisticated investors.

When there is mispricing, two possible sources of mispricings are: (1) the combinations of overreaction, underreaction, reversal, and momentum, and (2) bubbles and bursts. Unrealistic expectations of continued growth, which led to excessively high P/E ratios, caused the tech bubble in the late 1990s. High earnings that were not sustainable caused the credit bubble a decade later. Thus, in the latter case, it was not that the P/E ratios were too high, but that the earnings in the ratio eventually had to fall.

1. Which of the following are properties that should lead to firms having higher value in the stock market?
   I. Higher P/E.
   II. First-in first-out (FIFO) accounting.
   III. Higher growth.
   IV. ROIC greater than the cost of capital.
      A. I and II only.
      B. I, II, and III only.
      C. III and IV only.
      D. II, III, and IV only.
2. Which two of the following situations will create the most value?
   I. A high-ROIC company increasing P/E.
   II. A high-growth company increasing P/E.
   III. A high-ROIC company increasing growth.
   IV. A high-growth company increasing ROIC.
      A. I and II only.
      B. I and III only.
      C. II and III only.
      D. III and IV only.
3. According to Exhibit 5.5 in the text, which is true of the two sectors with the highest and next to highest market-value/capital ratio?
   I. Their market-value/earnings ratios were the highest and next to highest, respectively.
   II. Their ROICs were the highest and next to highest, respectively.
   III. Their growth rates were the highest and third highest, respectively.
   IV. Their P/E ratios were the highest and next to highest, respectively.
      A. I and II only.
      B. I and IV only.
      C. II and III only.
      D. II, III, and IV only.
4. The point of Exhibit 5.12 in the text is to show:
   A. That even the companies with the lowest earnings volatility do not have smooth earnings.
   B. The negative relationship between earnings volatility and returns to shareholders.
   C. The positive relationship between earnings volatility and returns to shareholders.

D. The significant change in stock returns that occurs when the managers of a company engage in earnings smoothing.

5. Academic research has found that share prices of companies that are removed from a major stock index:
   A. Trend down until significant news arrives to reverse the trend.
   B. Do not experience any abnormal returns either in the short term or in the long term.
   C. Drop immediately and then begin trading normally.
   D. Drop immediately, but the decline is usually reversed within one or two months.
6. Which of the following are valid reasons that cross-listing might actually improve a company's stock performance?
   I. Improved corporate governance.
   II. Trading in multiple time zones.
   III. Access to an increased number of investors.
   IV. Affirmation effect of being listed in more than one developed market.
      A. I, II, and IV only.
      B. I and III only.
      C. II and III only.
      D. II, III, and IV only.
7. Which of the following are valid reasons that a firm's stock split can be followed by an increase in the value of the shares of that firm?
   I. Signaling.
   II. Liquidity.
   III. More shares outstanding.
   IV. Self-selection.
      A. I and IV only.
      B. II and III only.
      C. II, III, and IV only.
      D. None of these.
8. Voluntary option expensing has been found to have which of the following?
   A. A negative impact on share price.
   B. A positive impact on share price.
   C. No impact on share price.
   D. A positive impact if LIFO accounting is used and a negative effect if FIFO accounting is used.

9. An analysis of 50 European companies that began reporting using U.S. GAAP over the period 1997 to 2004 found which of the following?
   I. Earnings under GAAP were generally lower than earnings under the home country's rules.
   II. The differences in earnings under the two regimes were all less than 10 percent.
   III. The stocks of the 50 companies generally reacted positively when the disclosures were made.
   IV. Executives had concerns over the impact of reporting under U.S. GAAP.

   A. I and II only.
   B. I, II, and III only.
   C. I, III, and IV only.
   D. II, III, and IV only.
10. The effect of goodwill amortization on share prices has been found to be:
    A. Positive and significant overall.
    B. Negative and significant overall.
    C. Insignificant.
11. (True/False): Random deviations from intrinsic value can occur in stock prices, but managers are best off assuming that the market will correctly reflect the intrinsic value of their decisions.
12. Both the 2001 bubble and the 2007 bubble were valuation bubbles.
13. Market-wide price deviations from fair value are less frequent than individual company share price deviations from the company's fundamental value.
14. In the 1999 stock bubble, most of the large-capitalization companies with high P/Es were clustered in all of the following sectors *except*:
    A. Utilities.
    B. Technology.
    C. Media.
    D. Telecommunications.
15. Which of the following was *not* one of the faster growing sectors in the period 2000–2006?
    A. The energy sector.
    B. The financial sector.
    C. The transportation sector.
    D. The utilities sector.

16. Which of the following is/are correct concerning how managers should perceive short-term volatility of their stock?
    I. See it as a sign of market inefficiency.
    II. Take it into account when driving ROIC.
    III. Take it into account when driving growth.
    IV. Investors offer no rewards for predictable earnings or earnings guidance.
    Note that it will be higher when there is more uncertainty.
    A. I, II, and III only.
    B. I and IV only.
    C. II and III only.
    D. IV only.
17. The title of "informed trader" would most aptly apply to:
    A. Intrinsic investors.
    B. Traders.
    C. Quants.
    D. Indexers.
18. Which of the following characterize noise traders?
    I. They do not care about intrinsic value.
    II. They are always in the minority.
    III. They can move price outside the bounds of intrinsic value.
    IV. They trade on small events.
    A. I and II only.
    B. I, III, and IV only.
    C. II, III, and IV only.
    D. II and IV only.

6

Return on Invested Capital

The basic source of value creation is competitive advantage. The following expression expands the expression of ROIC proposed in Chapter 2:

$$\text{ROIC} = \frac{\text{NOPLAT}}{\text{Invested Capital}} = (1 - \text{Tax Rate})\frac{\text{Price per Unit} - \text{Cost per Unit}}{\text{Invested Capital per Unit}}$$

This formula explains how a higher ROIC is the result of a competitive advantage from being able to charge a higher price or being able to produce at a lower cost. The structure-conduct-performance (SCP) framework provides a strategy model for competitive advantage. One of the most widely used approaches in analyzing strategy is Porter's framework, which focuses on threat of entry, pressure from substitute products, bargaining power of buyers, bargaining power of suppliers, and the degree of rivalry among existing competitors. These forces differ widely by industry.

Five pricing advantages and four cost advantages determine overall competitive advantage. The five pricing advantages are innovative products, quality, brand, customer lock-in, and rational price discipline. The four cost advantages are innovative business methods, unique resources, economies of scale, and scalable products/processes. In a competitive economy, the pricing and cost advantages can erode through competition, and the sustainability of the high ROIC from a competitive advantage depends on issues such as the length of the life cycle of the business and the potential for renewing products. The evidence shows that the relative ROIC of a firm to the average of all other firms and to the firms in the industry remains fairly sustainable for periods of 10 years or more; however, there will be some reversion to the median and/or mean.

1. List Michael Porter's five forces:

   A. ____.

   B. ____.

C. ____.

D. ____.

E. ____.

2. The key driver of ROIC is ____________________.
3. According to empirical studies over the past five decades, how successful have firms been in sustaining their rates of ROIC?
4. Explain what quality means in the context of competitive advantage and ROIC.
5. For a pricing advantage, using rational pricing discipline requires either a ____________________ or ____________________.
6. Explain the difference between economies of scale and scalable products.
7. Between 1963 and the early 2000s, the median ROIC was about ____________ percent, and the interquartile range was from ____________ percent to ____________ percent.
8. Since the early 2000s, the median ROIC was about ____________ percent, and the interquartile range was from ____________ percent to ____________ percent.
9. The increase in median ROIC and the widening of the distribution of ROICs are the result of ____________________.
10. The reason for the increasing difference between ROIC without goodwill and ROIC including goodwill is ____________________.
11. From highest to lowest, rank the following three industries based on ROIC. They have been selected based on branding advantages and barriers to entry.

A. Paper, forest products	1. __________
B. Pharmaceuticals	2. __________
C. Consumer staples	3. __________
D. Health care equipment, supplies	4. __________

12. If a firm establishes itself as a high-ROIC firm, within 10 years it is expected that the ROIC will:

A. Have fallen to the average or be below the average ROIC.

B. Have fallen, but will still be above the average ROIC.

C. Not have fallen, and will maintain about the same.

D. Have continued to trend up.

13. Given that a company charges $3.40 per unit, has a cost per unit of $1.80, has a tax rate of 32 percent, and requires $16 of invested capital per unit, what is the ROIC?
    A. 6.8 percent.
    B. 10.2 percent.
    C. 15.6 percent.
    D. 30.3 percent.
14. Cereal manufacturers have been successful at branding their products, while meat producers have been unable to do so to a large degree. Based on this fact, which of the following is the most accurate concerning the pricing advantage that cereal manufacturers have over meat producers?
    A. The ROIC for cereal manufacturers is less than that of meat producers because branding does not create value and branding has a cost.
    B. The ROIC for cereal manufacturers is equal to that of meat producers because the costs and benefits reach an equilibrium.
    C. The ROIC for cereal manufacturers is twice as high as that of meat producers.
    D. The ROIC for cereal manufacturers is three times as high as that of meat producers.

7

Growth

Growth can vary greatly across industries and across firms within industries. There are three components of revenue growth: (1) portfolio momentum, (2) market share performance, and (3) mergers and acquisitions. Components (1) and (2) are types of organic growth. Components (1) and (3) have the highest explanatory power. In other words, high growth depends more on choosing the right markets and acquisitions and less on gaining market share.

The highest value-creating strategy is entering into fast-growing markets that take revenue from distant companies instead of rivals in the local industry. Other value-creating strategies include developing new products or services, persuading customers to increase the use of existing products, and attracting new customers.

Trying to increase market share in a growing market may have some success, but it will probably fail to create value in a mature market because of the reactions of rivals. Product promotions, pricing promotions, and incremental product changes rarely create lasting value.

Since products have natural life cycles, sustaining growth is more difficult than sustaining ROIC. To sustain growth, a firm must consistently develop new products in a timely fashion. A study of publicly traded companies found that over the period 1965 to 2013, the median revenue growth rate was 5.3 percent, and the range of the growth rates was 0 percent to 9 percent. High growth rates decay quickly, and large companies struggle to grow. The median growth of publicly traded companies exceeded that of U.S. gross domestic product (GDP) for four possible reasons: (1) greater access to capital, (2) the effects of outsourcing, (3) expansion into foreign markets, and (4) the fact that GDP is driven more by larger firms, which grow more slowly than the median firm in the sample.

1. Identify the sources of organic growth and indicate which has the highest explanatory power for growth.

2. Explain the importance of incremental innovation in creating value.
3. With respect to product development, growth is difficult to maintain because for each product ______________, the company must ______________. This is called the ______________ effect.
4. How has the growth of publicly traded companies in the United States compared to the growth of U.S. GDP?

   Explain the two reasons for the difference.

   A. ____.

   B. ____.
5. Which of the following is most accurate concerning the median revenue growth rates of firms over the years 1965 to 2013?
   A. The range was 1.5 percent to 12 percent, with a median of 7.2 percent.
   B. The range was 0 percent to 9 percent, with a median of 5.3 percent.
   C. The range was 2.2 percent to 8.8 percent, with a median of 4.2 percent.
   D. The range was –0.2 percent to 6.6 percent, with a median of 3.3 percent.
6. Companies that grow faster than 30 percent in one year generally within five years see their growth decline to:
   A. About 4 percent and then down to 2 percent within 10 years.
   B. About 12 percent and then down to 10 percent within 10 years.
   C. About 10 percent and then down to 8 percent within 10 years.
   D. About 8 percent and then down to 6 percent within 10 years.
7. Companies that grow slower than 0 percent in one year generally within five years see their growth increase to:
   A. About 4 percent and then up to 4.5 percent within 10 years.
   B. About 1 percent and then up to 2 percent within 10 years.
   C. About 6 percent and then up to 8 percent within 10 years.
   D. About 8 percent and then up to 10 percent within 10 years.
8. Which of the following explain the reasons that growth-rate rankings change among industries so much over time?

   I. The business cycle.

   II. Changing regulations.

   III. Fluctuating exchange rates.

   IV. Product life cycles.

   A. I and II only.

   B. I and IV only.

C. II and III only.

D. III and IV only.

9. Which of the following is true concerning an increase in market share that comes at the expense of established competitors?

   A. It rarely creates much value for long, except when it results in pushing a competitor out of the market completely.

   B. It generally creates value for a fairly long period, but it will decay after about 10 years.

   C. It never creates any value over the long run because the effects are random across firms and net to zero for any given firm over time.

   D. None of these.

10. Which of the following usually result in above-average value creation?

    I. Make large acquisitions.

    II. Attract new customers into the market.

    III. Convince existing customers to buy more of a product.

    IV. Make bolt-on acquisitions to accelerate product growth.

    A. I and II only.

    B. I, III, and IV only.

    C. II and III only.

    D. III and IV only.

11. For firms that grew at rates less than 5 percent in the 2000–2003 period, what percent grew at rates greater than 10 percent in the 2010–2013 period?

    A. 44 percent.

    B. 15 percent.

    C. 13 percent.

    D. 28 percent.

12. For firms that grew at rates greater than 15 percent in the 2000–2003 period, what percent grew at rates less than 10 percent in the 2010–2013 period?

    A. 58 percent.

    B. 37 percent.

    C. 21 percent.

    D. 42 percent.

8

Frameworks for Valuation

Two popular methods for estimating the value of a company are the discounted cash flow (DCF) model and the discounted economic-profit model. Both methods use WACC in the discounting process, and both should give the same estimate. They are appropriate if the capital structure is expected to remain stable; but if the capital structure will change, then the adjusted present value (APV) model is a good alternative. Alternatives to discounted cash flow models include using multiples and real-option models.

To value the firm's equity using the DCF model, an analyst estimates the value of the operating assets, adds the value of nonoperating assets (e.g., cash), and then subtracts the value of debt. An estimate of the value of operations requires a reorganization of financial statements; an analysis of historical performance; a projection of revenue growth, ROIC, and free cash flow; an estimate of continuing value (CV); and an appropriate discount rate.

Economic-profit-based valuation models have the advantage of providing insights into the yearly performance. One formula for economic profit is:

$$\text{Economic Profit} = \text{NOPLAT} - (\text{Invested Capital} \times \text{WACC})$$

If economic profit grows at a constant rate, the value of a firm can be expressed as:

$$\text{Value}_0 = \text{Invested Capital}_0 + \text{Economic Profit}_1/(\text{WACC} - g)$$

If forecasts predict that the capital structure of a firm will change (e.g., the firm pays down debt over time), the adjusted present value (APV) model is the best choice. The APV model uses the following breakdown to value the firm:

$$\begin{aligned}\text{Adjusted Present Value} = {} & \text{Enterprise Value as If All} - \text{Equity Financed} \\ & + \text{Present Value of Tax Shields}\end{aligned}$$

The first component of APV, the enterprise value as if the company were all-equity financed, is determined by discounting the cash flows using the unlevered cost of equity.

1. The estimate of a firm's present value (PV) of free cash flows (FCFs) is $400 million. Its estimated invested capital is $700 million. It has cash holdings of $9 million. The value of debt and capitalized operating leases are $220 million and $33 million, respectively. If there are 2 million shares of common equity outstanding, what is the estimated value of each share?
2. A firm's estimated present value of economic profit is $150 million. Its estimated invested capital is $250 million. It has cash holdings of $16 million. The value of debt and capitalized operating leases are $80 million and $26 million, respectively. What is the estimated value of equity?
3. Which of the following valuation methods does *not* assume the WACC is constant?
   A. The discounted cash flow model.
   B. The economic-profit model.
   C. The adjusted present value model.
   D. None of these. They all assume the WACC is constant.
4. Which of the following is *not* a nonequity claim against the value of the firm?
   A. Tax loss carried forward.
   B. Unfunded retirement liabilities.
   C. Preferred stock.
   D. Minority interest.
5. The value of a firm's invested capital is $300 million. Its return on invested capital is 12 percent, and its WACC is 10.5 percent. What is the economic profit?
6. Explain the relationship of the adjusted present value model to the Modigliani and Miller proposition concerning the effect of a firm's capital structure on the value of the firm.
7. Complete the table:

Source of capital	Proportion of total capital	Cost of capital	Marginal tax rate	After-tax cost of capital	Contribution to WACC
Debt	42%	6.2%	34%		
Equity	58%	9.8%			
WACC					

8. For the next period, a firm's free cash flow (FCF) and its interest tax shield (ITS) are estimated to be $40 million and $9 million, respectively. Their growth rates are estimated to be 5 percent and 3 percent, respectively. The unlevered cost of equity is 9 percent and the cost of debt is 6 percent. The levered cost of equity is 12 percent. Using the capital cash flow model, what is the estimated value of the firm?

9. Suppose that it is December 31, 2016. Fill in the following table to calculate equity value. The discount rate is 9 percent. (Hint: See Exhibit 8.14 in the text.)

Year	Free cash flow (FCF)	Interest tax shield (ITS)	Discount factor	PV of FCF	PV of ITS
2016	402	31			
2017	420	32			
2018	436	34			
Continuing value	8,900	380			
Present value					
PV of free cash flow					
PV of interest tax shield					
PV of free cash flow and interest tax shield					
Midyear adjustment factor					
Value of operations					
Value of long-term investments	155				
Value of tax loss carry-forwards	81				
Enterprise value					
Value of debt	2,583				
Value of capitalized operating leases	1,674				
Equity value					

9

Reorganizing the Financial Statements

A proper assessment of financial performance requires reorganizing financial statements to avoid traps like double counting, omitting cash flows, and hiding leverage. A key measure of economic performance is net operating profit less adjusted taxes (NOPLAT), because ROIC = NOPLAT/(Invested capital), and FCF = NOPLAT + Noncash operating expenses – Investments in invested capital.

Other important measures are:

$$\text{Invested Capital} = \text{Operating Assets} - \text{Operating Liabilities} = \text{Debt} + \text{Equity}$$

for a simplistic firm, and

$$\begin{aligned}\text{Total Funds Invested} &= \text{Invested Capital} + \text{Nonoperating Assets}\\ &= (\text{Debt and Debt Equivalents})\\ &\quad + (\text{Equity and Equity Equivalents})\end{aligned}$$

for a more realistic firm.

In practice, there are difficulties in categorizing assets as operating or nonoperating and right-hand balance sheet items as debt or equity, and this makes computing the values in these equations difficult. The analyst should not include excess cash in invested capital because it is not necessary for core operations, and including it will depress ROIC. Also, if a company has financial subsidiaries, the operations of those subsidiaries require a separate analysis from those of the manufacturing operations, because financial institutions have different capital and leverage norms.

Advanced analytical issues include operating leases, pensions and other retirement benefits, capitalized research and development, and nonoperating charges and restructuring reserves. An analyst can estimate the implied value of those leased assets that are not capitalized and obtain a more appropriate measure of leverage with the following equation:

$$\text{Asset Value}_{t-1} = \frac{\text{Rental Expense}_t}{k_d + \frac{1}{\text{Asset Life}}}$$

Like excess cash, excess pension assets and pension shortfalls should not be included in invested capital. Research and development should be included in invested capital. Provisions fall into four basic categories: ongoing operating provisions, long-term operating provisions, nonoperating provisions, and income-smoothing provisions. Each requires an adjustment to return or invested capital or both.

1. How will an increase in invested capital affect FCF and ROIC if all other things are kept equal?
   A. It will decrease both FCF and ROIC.
   B. It will increase both FCF and ROIC.
   C. It will increase FCF but decrease ROIC.
   D. It will decrease FCF but increase ROIC.
2. Which of the following are sources of financing?
   I. Equity equivalents.
   II. Debt equivalents.
   III. Hybrid securities.
   IV. Noncontrolling interest.
      A. I and II only.
      B. I, II, and III only.
      C. III and IV only.
      D. I, II, III, and IV.
3. For which of the following would the tax assets and liabilities *not* be included in operating deferred-tax assets or liabilities?
   A. Accelerated inventory deduction.
   B. Goodwill and other intangibles.
   C. Accrued self-insurance liabilities.
   D. State income taxes.
4. In calculating free cash flows, which of the following are *not* an investment that should be subtracted from gross cash flows?

A. Change in operating working capital.
B. Change in debt outstanding.
C. Net capital expenditures.
D. Investment in goodwill and acquired intangibles.

5. For a given leased asset using an operating lease, the rental expense will be $5,000 in the next period. The pretax cost of debt is 8 percent, and the asset has an expected life of five years. When adjusting the balance sheet for estimating value, what would be the estimated asset value of the leased asset in the current period?
   A. $12,500
   B. $50,000
   C. $17,857
   D. $38,462
6. A firm's balance sheet has the following entries: cash = $200, receivables = $100, short-term deferred tax assets = $30, and short-term deferred tax liabilities = $10. The firm has revenues of $5,000. Based on this information, what is the value of operating current assets?
   A. $200
   B. $300
   C. $330
   D. $340
7. According to FASB Statement 158 under U.S. Generally Accepted Accounting Principles (GAAP), with respect to pension value shortfalls and excess pension assets, which are reported directly on the balance sheet?
   A. The present value of pension value shortfalls only.
   B. The present value of both pension value shortfalls and excess pension assets.
   C. The undiscounted value of pension value shortfalls only.
   D. The undiscounted value of pension value shortfalls and the present value of pension assets.
8. Given the following balance sheet entries, compute the debt and the total funds invested.

Operating assets = $400	Accounts payable = $60
Marketable securities = $100	Prepaid pension assets = $50
Deferred taxes = $30	Common stock = $200

9. Given the following accounting income statement on the left, enter the appropriate entries into the NOPLAT worksheet on the right. The marginal tax rate is 30 percent.

Revenues	$2,000	Revenues	$2,000
Operating costs	(1,000)	Operating costs	(1,000)
Depreciation	(400)	Depreciation	(400)
Operating profit	$600	Operating profit	$600
Interest	(40)	Operating taxes	
Nonoperating income	10	NOPLAT	
Earnings before taxes	$570	After-tax nonoperating income	
Taxes	(171)	Income available to investors	
Net income	$399		

10. Given the following financial statements, calculate NOPLAT, working capital, invested capital, and total funds invested.

Income statement	**Year**	**Balance sheet**	**Year**
Revenues	200.0	Working cash	10
Cost of sales	(80.0)	Accounts receivable	30
Selling costs	(50.0)	Inventories	10
Depreciation	(20.0)	Current assets	50
Operating profit	50.0		
		Property, plant, and equipment	150
Interest expense	(4.0)	Prepaid pension assets	5
Gain on sale	–	Total assets	205
Earnings before taxes	46.0		
		Accounts payable	6
Taxes	(13.8)	Short-term debt	12
Net income	32.2	Restructuring reserves	7
		Current liabilities	25
Operating tax rate = 30%			
Marginal tax rate = 30%		Long-term debt	70
		Shareholders' equity	110
		Liabilities and equity	205

10

Analyzing Performance

The analysis of performance and competitive position begins with an analysis of the key drivers of value: ROIC and revenue growth. After that analysis, an assessment of the financial health of the firm shows whether it can make short-term and long-term investments.

It is useful to analyze ROIC with and without goodwill. Also, the following breakdown of ROIC is a powerful equation in financial analysis:

$$\text{ROIC} = (1 - \text{Operating Cash Tax Rate}) \times \frac{\text{EBITA}}{\text{Revenues}} \times \frac{\text{Revenues}}{\text{Invested Capital}}$$

Revenue growth is one of the determinants of cash flows. The analyst should distinguish between organic revenue growth and growth from other factors such as currency effects, acquisitions, or divestitures.

A comprehensive model does a line item analysis, which converts every line in the financial statements into a ratio. Ratios include common size entries computed in terms of assets or revenues for the balance sheet and income statement, respectively, and also days ratios found by the following general expression:

$$\text{Days} = 365 \times \frac{\text{Balance Sheet Item}}{\text{Revenues}}$$

Other measures provide insights into efficiency relative to other firms. One such expression is a breakdown of labor costs per unit:

$$\frac{\text{Labor Expenses}}{\text{Units of Output}} = \frac{\text{Labor Expenses/Number of Employees}}{\text{Units of Output/Number of Employees}}$$

The following equation helps illustrate the power and danger of leverage:

$$\text{ROE} = \text{ROIC} + [\text{ROIC} - (1 - T) \times k_d] \times \text{D/E}$$

The analyst should note how the market debt-to-equity ratio compares to peers in terms of the coverage and the level of risk the firm takes.

1. Explain why ROIC is a better analytical tool than return on equity (ROE) and return on assets (ROA).

   ROE: ____________

   ROA: ____________

2. Which of the following is most accurate?
   A. Analyzing ROIC excluding goodwill is the best measure for determining value added for shareholders.
   B. Analyzing ROIC excluding goodwill serves no purpose.
   C. Analyzing ROIC excluding goodwill is the preferred method for most analysis.
   D. None of these statements are true.
3. Compute ROIC given the following information: EBITA = $3,000, Revenues = $24,000, Invested capital = $20,000, Operating cash tax rate = 25 percent.
   A. 3.75 percent.
   B. 5.33 percent.
   C. 11.25 percent.
   D. 18.75 percent.
4. Compute operating profit margin and capital turnover given the following information: EBITA = $3,000, Revenues = $24,000, Invested capital = $20,000, Operating cash tax rate = 25 percent.
   A. 12.5 percent; 1.2.
   B. 15.0 percent; 1.2.
   C. 15.0 percent; 0.8.
   D. 12.5 percent; 0.8.
5. Which of the following is the best method of determining if the financial performance between competitors is sustainable?
   A. Linking operating drivers directly to return on capital.
   B. Comparing the respective ROE and ROA measures.
   C. Breaking ROE down into ROIC, tax, interest rate, and leverage effects.
   D. Distinguishing between pretax ROIC and operating-cash tax rate.

6. Given that ROIC, the interest rate on debt, and the debt-to-equity ratio are constant, how will increasing the tax rate affect ROE?
   A. Decrease it.
   B. Not affect it.
   C. Increase it.
   D. There is no set relationship.
7. In Exhibit 10.3 in the text, pretax ROIC is broken down into:
   A. Operating margin and operating-cash tax rate.
   B. Operating margin and revenues divided by invested capital.
   C. Operating working capital divided by revenues and fixed assets divided by revenues.
   D. Gross margin and selling, general, and administrative (SG&A) expense divided by revenues.
8. Other things being constant, if EBITA and revenues both increase by 10 percent, then it is likely that:
   A. ROIC will decrease.
   B. ROIC will remain the same.
   C. ROIC will increase.
   D. ROIC will change, but the direction is not certain.

Use the following data to answer Questions 9 and 10.

	2015	2016
Current assets	$863	$896
Current liabilities	710	818
Debt in current liabilities	1	39
Long-term debt	506	408
Total assets	2,293	2,307
Capital expenditures	111	117
Change in deferred taxes	–29	–20
Sales	4,056	4,192
Operating expenses	3,307	3,260
Rental expense	0	248
General expenses	562	528
Depreciation	139	136
Interest expense	39	30
Income taxes	5	8

9. For each year, compute the three coverage ratios based on pretax and interest income.

2015	Ratio 1	Ratio 2	Ratio 3
Numerator			
Denominator			
Ratio			
2016	**Ratio 1**	**Ratio 2**	**Ratio 3**
Numerator			
Denominator			
Ratio			

10. If receivables, inventories, and other current assets are $523 in 2015, then what is the number of days in cash?

11

Forecasting Performance

Typically, forecasting involves making projections of cash flows to some point where the company has a steady state going forward characterized by two properties: (1) the company grows at a constant rate with a constant reinvestment ratio, and (2) the company earns a constant rate of return on existing capital and new capital invested. The horizon to the steady state, called the explicit forecast period, is usually 10 to 15 years. The analyst should divide the explicit forecast period into a first forecast period of five to seven years, where the statements will include many details, and the remaining years' forecasts where the statements are simpler with less detail, which avoids the error of false precision. Such forecasts require assumptions concerning a host of variables, including the return earned on invested capital and whether the company can stay competitive.

There are six steps in the forecasting process.

1. Prepare and analyze historical financial statements and data.
2. Build the revenue forecast consistent with historical economy-wide evidence on growth.
3. Forecast the income statement using the appropriate economic drivers.
4. Forecast the balance sheet entries.
5. Forecast the investor funds into the balance sheet.
6. Calculate ROIC and FCF.

Additional issues include determining the effect of inflation, nonfinancial drivers, and which costs are fixed and which are variable.

For Questions 1 through 5, answer True or False.

1. When using plant, property, and equipment (PP&E) as the forecast driver, tie depreciation to net PP&E, rather than using a gross PP&E approach.

2. It is recommended in the financial modeling process to collect raw data on a separate worksheet and record the data as originally reported.
3. The top-down approach cannot be applied to companies in mature industries.
4. The recommended method to forecast taxes is as a percentage of earnings before taxes.
5. To forecast the balance sheet, it is best to first forecast invested capital and nonoperating assets and then forecast excess cash and sources of financing separately.
6. Which of the following is *not* one of the steps in the forecast of individual line items related to the income statement?

   A. Determine the economic relationships that drive the model.

   B. Model the business cycle.

   C. Estimate the forecast ratios.

   D. Forecast the drivers and multiply times the respective ratios.
7. If a company forecasts that its capital expenditures will be smooth, then which is the better method to use for forecasting depreciation: (i) using a percentage of revenues or (ii) using a percentage of property, plant, and equipment?

   A. Percentage of revenues only.

   B. Percentage of property, plant, and equipment only.

   C. Either method is appropriate because the choice does not matter if expenditures are smooth.

   D. Neither method is appropriate when expenditures are smooth.
8. Which of the following is the best estimate of retained earnings in year T?

   A. Retained earnings$_{T-1}$ + Net income$_{T-1}$ – Dividends$_T$

   B. Retained earnings$_T$ + Net income$_{T-1}$ – Dividends$_{T-1}$

   C. Retained earnings$_{T-1}$ + Net income$_T$ – Dividends$_T$

   D. Retained earnings$_T$ + Net income$_T$ + Dividends$_T$
9. In industries where prices are changing or technology is advancing, forecasters should:

   A. Use only financial drivers such as revenue.

   B. Use only nonfinancial drivers such as productivity and volume.

   C. Use both financial and nonfinancial drivers.

   D. Use national real aggregates such as real GDP.
10. The value of a steady-state company:

    A. Can be estimated by estimating free cash flow and using the growth perpetuity model.

B. Can be estimated using the quadratic formula.

C. Can be estimated using the PP&E method.

D. Cannot be estimated because at zero growth, the solution involves division by zero.

11. Explain the problem with respect to forecasting cash flows of a parent company that are from investments in subsidiaries where the parent owns less than 20 percent of the subsidiary.

12. List the three steps in making a top-down forecast of revenue:

    A. ______________________________.

    B. ______________________________.

    C. ______________________________.

    List the three inputs for making a bottom-up forecast of revenue:

    A. ______________________________.

    B. ______________________________.

    C. ______________________________.

13. Complete the following table by entering the typical forecast driver in the third column and the typical forecast ratio in the last column.

Typical forecast drivers for the income statement	Line item	Typical forecast driver	Typical forecast ratio
Operating	Cost of goods sold (COGS)		
	Selling, general, and administrative expense		
	Depreciation		
Nonoperating	Interest expense		
	Interest income		

14. At the beginning of the year 2015, an analyst has the information in the following table concerning income for 2015. Assume all income is taxed at the same indicated tax rate. The balance sheet assumptions for 2015 are:

    A. Operating cash, excess cash, and equity investments will not change.

    B. Inventory, net PP&E, and accounts payable will increase at the same rate as sales.

    C. Short-term and long-term debt will increase by 10 percent. There will be no equity issuance nor repurchase of shares.

D. The firm will use a residual dividend policy, so that all additional financing will come from retained earnings and the rest of earnings will be paid out as a dividend.

Fill out the table.

	2015	2016		2015	2016
Revenue growth		20%	Revenues	500	600
Cost of goods sold/revenue	40%	40%	Cost of goods sold		
Selling and general expenses/revenues	30%	20%	Selling and general expenses		
Depreciation/net PP&E	20%	30%	Depreciation	(56)	
EBITA/revenues			EBITA		
Interest rate					
Interest expense/ total debt	10%	8%	Interest expense	(40)	
Interest income/ excess cash	6%	5%	Interest income	12	
			Nonoperating income	10	
Nonoperating items			Earnings before taxes		
Nonoperating income growth		30%			
			Provision for income taxes	(22.8)	
Taxes			Net income		
Average tax rate	30%	30%			
	2014	**2015**		**2014**	**2015**
Assets			Liabilities and equity		
Operating cash	10		Accounts payable	20	
Excess cash	200		Short-term debt	300	
Inventory	60		Current liabilities	320	
Current assets	270				
			Long-term debt	100	
Net PP&E	280		Common stock	80	
Equity investments	100		Retained earnings	150	
Total assets	650		Total liabilities and equity	650	

12

Estimating Continuing Value

There are two parts to the estimated value of a company based on future cash flows: (1) a portion of the value based on the initial, explicit forecast period, and (2) a portion of the value based on continuing performance beginning at the end of the explicit forecast period. The continuing value (CV) often exceeds half of the total estimated operating value, and when early years have negative cash flows, the continuing value can exceed the total estimated operating value. There are two formulas for estimating continuing value: (1) the discounted cash flow (DCF) formula and (2) the economic-profit formula. The DCF formula is:

$$CV_t = \frac{NOPLAT_{t+1}\left[1 - \frac{g}{RONIC}\right]}{WACC - g}$$

Special considerations in estimating the inputs are that (1) NOPLAT should reflect an average level associated with the midpoint of the business cycle, (2) return on new invested capital (RONIC) should reflect realistic assumptions concerning the level of competition, (3) WACC should be based on a sustainable capital structure, and (4) g should be based on a long-term measure such as the consumption growth for the industry's products.

The economic-profit formula for continuing value is:

$$CV_t = \frac{IC_t[ROIC_t - WACC]}{WACC} + \frac{PV(\text{Economic Profit}_{t+2})}{WACC - g}$$

$$PV(\text{Economic Profit}_{t+2}) = \frac{NOPLAT_{t+1}\left(\frac{g}{RONIC}\right)(RONIC - WACC)}{WACC}$$

The length of the explicit forecast period does not affect the value of the company. There can be a difference between the return on new invested capital and the return on existing invested capital. Also, there is not necessarily a direct relationship between the size of the estimated continuing value and the actual value created in the continuing value period.

Other methods for estimating continuing value exist. The convergence formula is related to the preceding formulas, for example, and it assumes that excess profits will eventually be competed away. The convergence formula gives the following relationship:

$$CV_t = \frac{NOPLAT_{t+1}}{WACC}$$

Some methods do not depend on the time value of money. Those methods include using multiples such as P/E, estimates of liquidation value, and estimates of replacement costs.

For Questions 1 through 5, answer True or False.

1. The expected long-term rate of consumption growth for the industry's products plus inflation is a good estimate for growth in the continuing value models.
2. The estimate of continuing value after the explicit forecast period cannot be higher than the total value of the firm.
3. Analysts are usually overly optimistic about continuing value.
4. In a growing, profitable industry, a company's liquidation value is probably well below the going concern value.
5. The percentage of the firm's value determined by continuing value would most likely increase as the forecast horizon increases.
6. As a firm begins to grow and faces increasing competition as it expands, which of the following is most likely to be the relationships among ROIC on base capital, RONIC, and ROIC on total capital?

   A. ROIC on base capital < RONIC < ROIC on total capital.

   B. ROIC on base capital > RONIC > ROIC on total capital.

   C. ROIC on base capital > ROIC on total capital > RONIC.

   D. ROIC on base capital < ROIC on total capital < RONIC.

7. An analyst makes a five-year explicit forecast of revenues of a firm. During those five years, the firm is expected to grow between 10 and 12 percent per year. After that, the growth rate is expected to level off at 8 percent. Should the analyst use a naive base-year extrapolation for the continuing value estimation? Why or why not?

   A. No, because it will likely underestimate free cash flow.

   B. No, because it will likely overestimate free cash flow.

C. Yes, because it is the most proven method under the given circumstances.

D. Yes, because it is the most proven method in all circumstances.

8. The alternative continuing value measure $CV_t = (NOPLAT_{t+1})/WACC$ depends on the assumption that:

A. Excess profits will be competed away.

B. WACC is greater than the inflation rate.

C. $NOPLAT_{t+1}$ represents a value from the peak of the business cycle.

D. $NOPLAT_{t+1}$ represents a value from the trough of the business cycle.

9. Which of the following have a positive relationship with economic profit?

I. Growth.

II. RONIC.

III. WACC.

IV. NOPLAT.

A. I and II only.

B. I, II, and IV only.

C. I, III, and IV only.

D. II, III, and IV only.

10. Exhibit 12.9 in the text illustrates how the value of a firm can be broken down into two or more subparts. Which of the following is *not* one of those breakdowns?

A. Nonoperating assets and (2) operating assets plus the present value of the depreciation tax shield.

B. New product line and (2) base business.

C. Present value of continuing value cash flow and (2) the present value of the cash flow from the explicit forecast period.

D. The present value of economic profit from continuing value, (2) the present value of economic profit of the explicit forecast period, and (3) invested capital.

11. List and explain the three non-cash-flow approaches to valuation.

A. ______________.

B. ______________.

C. ______________.

12. If $NOPLAT_{t+1}$ = \$200, g = 4 percent, RONIC = 10 percent, WACC = 8 percent, then what is continuing value in year t?

13. An analyst is estimating the continuing value after the explicit forecast period using the economic-profit formula. The analyst estimates that

invested capital at the end of the explicit forecast period will be $2,000 and the ROIC on existing capital after the explicit forecast period will be 12 percent. NOPLAT in the year following the explicit forecast period is expected to be $240 and is expected to grow at 2 percent per year. The RONIC is expected to be 10 percent, and the cost of capital is 7 percent. What is the continuing value (CV) after the explicit forecast period?

14. Fill in the following table and compute the value of operations, calculating the CV at the end of Year 3.

	Year 1	Year 2	Year 3	CV	Key value drivers	
Revenues	$200.0	$210.0	$216.0	$220.0	Investment rate	60.0%
Operating costs					Return on new capital	15.0%
Operating margin					Growth rate	9.0%
Operating taxes					Operating costs as percent of sales	90.0%
NOPLAT					Operating taxes	30.0%
					NOPLAT margin	7.0%
Net investment						
Free cash flow						
					ROIC	14.0%
Discounted cash flow					Cost of capital	12.0%
Discount rate						
Discounted cash flow						
Value of operations						

13

Estimating the Cost of Capital

The WACC is the opportunity cost of choosing to invest in the assets generating the free cash flow (FCF) of that business as opposed to another business of similar risk. For consistency, the estimate of the WACC should have the following properties: (1) it includes the opportunity cost of all investors, (2) it uses the appropriate market-based weights, (3) it includes related costs/benefits such as the interest tax shield, (4) it is computed after corporate taxes, (5) it is based on the same expectations of inflation as used in the FCF forecasts, and (6) the duration of the securities used in estimating the WACC equals the duration of the FCFs.

The estimation of WACC requires the estimate of inputs in the following equation:

$$\text{WACC} = \frac{D}{V}k_d(1 - T_m) + \frac{E}{V}k_e$$

Where D/V is the target weight in debt, E/V is the target weight in equity, k_i is the corresponding required return of each source of capital, and T_m is the marginal tax rate. The capital asset pricing model (CAPM) is a popular way to estimate of the cost of equity:

$$E(R_i) = r_f + \beta_i \times [E(R_m) - r_f]$$

which includes an estimate of the risk-free rate, beta, and the market risk premium. More than one way exists to estimate each of the inputs; there are alternatives to the CAPM such as the Fama-French three-factor model and the arbitrage pricing theory.

The after-tax cost of debt requires an estimate of the required return on debt capital and an estimate of the tax rate. Other estimates include the weights in the target capital structure and, when relevant, the effects of debt equivalents and the effects of a complex capital structure.

1. To estimate the risk-free rate in developed economies, the analyst should use:
   A. Short-term commercial paper.
   B. Short-term government discount instruments.
   C. Long-term coupon-paying government bonds.
   D. Long-term government zero-coupon bonds.
2. In computing the cost of equity for a firm, which of the following are recommended steps in estimating the CAPM beta using regression analysis?
   I. Use a sample size equal to or greater than 60.
   II. Use daily returns.
   III. Use a diversified value-weighted index.
   IV. Watch for possible distortions from market bubbles.
      A. I, II, and III only.
      B. I, III, and IV only.
      C. II and IV only.
      D. II, III, and IV only.
3. The weights to use in the WACC should reflect the:
   A. Current book values.
   B. Current market values.
   C. Target market-based values.
   D. Book values in the case of bonds and market values in the case of equity.
4. Which of the following is *not* an input into the Fama-French three-factor model?
   A. The difference between low book-to-market returns and high book-to-market returns.
   B. The difference between growth stock returns and value stock returns.
   C. The market portfolio returns.
   D. The difference between small-cap returns and large-cap returns.
5. Which of the following are true concerning the index recommended for use in the CAPM?

I. It should include both traded and untraded investments.
II. The S&P 500 is the most common proxy for U.S. stocks.
III. The S&P 500 and the MSCI World index will produce very different results for U.S. stocks.
IV. For less developed countries, a local market index is recommended.
   A. I and II.
   B. I and IV.
   C. II and III.
   D. III and IV.

6. Bloomberg's recommended adjustment to a firm's beta will:
   A. Lower beta in all cases.
   B. Increase beta in all cases.
   C. Move the beta toward one.
   D. Either increase or decrease beta, but it depends on the size of the standard error of the estimated beta.
7. Which of the following practices are appropriate in estimating a firm's cost of debt?
   I. Use the coupon rate on outstanding debt that is investment grade.
   II. Use the yield to maturity on outstanding debt that is investment grade.
   III. Use the yield to maturity on outstanding debt that is below investment grade.
   IV. Use the adjusted present value (APV) method to value firms that have debt that is below investment grade.
   A. I and IV only.
   B. II and IV only.
   C. II and III only.
   D. II and IV only.
8. What challenges did the financial crisis of 2008 and its aftermath pose for estimating a firm's cost of capital? How should one handle these challenges?
9. An analyst gathers the following information for Firm A and Firm B. Use the information to compute the industry unlevered beta and the appropriate beta for each company for use in the WACC. Assume that the debt beta for both firms equals zero.

   Firm A: CAPM beta = 0.7; debt-to-equity ratio = 0.4

   Firm B: CAPM beta = 1.2; debt-to-equity ratio = 2

10. A firm has a target debt-to-equity ratio of one. Its cost of equity equals 10 percent, the cost of debt is 6 percent, and the tax rate is 40 percent. What is the WACC?
11. A firm has 1,500,000 shares of stock outstanding with a price per share equal to $10. There are 8,000 bonds outstanding, priced at $1,125 each. The cost of equity is 12 percent, the cost of debt is 9 percent, and the corporate tax rate is 34 percent. What is the WACC?

14

Moving from Enterprise Value to Value per Share

Enterprise value is the value of the entire company, which equals the sum of core operations plus nonoperating assets. Subtracting debt, debt equivalents, and hybrid securities, and making other adjustments, provides an estimate of the value of equity. The value of equity divided by undiluted shares outstanding gives value per share. The process should avoid double counting and include valuations of interdependencies between the value of core operations and the value of nonoperating dependencies.

The valuation must carefully evaluate the nonoperating assets, which consist of excess cash and marketable securities, nonconsolidated subsidiaries and equity investments, loans to other companies, finance subsidiaries, discontinued operations, excess real estate, tax loss carryforwards, and excess pension assets. Debt and debt equivalents consist of debt of all kinds (for example, bonds, bank loans, and commercial paper); operating leases; securitized receivables; unfunded pension liabilities; contingent liabilities; and operating and nonoperating provisions. Hybrid securities consist of convertible debt and convertible preferred stock. Employee stock options and noncontrolling interests require additional adjustments.

1. Which of the following is *not* a method for evaluating convertible debt?
   A. Market value.
   B. Multiples valuation.
   C. Black-Scholes valuation.
   D. Conversion price valuation.
2. An analyst is applying an integrated-scenario approach to evaluate operations as well as equity, and the analyst essentially treats equity as

a call option on the enterprise value. It is most likely the analysis is of a company that:

A. Is highly levered.

B. Has securitized receivables.

C. Uses income smoothing.

D. Has excess pension assets or liabilities.

3. In evaluating employee stock options, the exercise value approach provides:

   A. A lower bound of valuation, and using it can undervalue the firm.

   B. An upper bound of valuation, and using it can undervalue the firm.

   C. A lower bound of valuation, and using it can overvalue the firm.

   D. A upper bound of valuation, and using it can overvalue the firm.

4. Company X controls Company Y so that Company Y's financial statements are fully consolidated in the group accounts. With respect to Company X's financial statements, third-party stakes in Company Y:

   A. Are not of concern.

   B. Are to be deducted and are called noncontrolling interest.

   C. Are to be added in and are called noncontrolling interest.

   D. Are illegal.

5. For equity stakes in subsidiaries where the stake is between 20 and 50 percent of the subsidiary, the holding is recorded on the balance sheet at:

   A. Market value, and the parent's portion of subsidiary's profits are shown below operating profit on the parent company's income statement.

   B. Historical cost plus reinvested income, and the parent's portion of subsidiary's profits are shown in the regular operating profit of the parent company.

   C. Market value, and the parent's portion of subsidiary's profits are shown in the regular operating profit of the parent company.

   D. Historical cost plus reinvested income, and the parent's portion of subsidiary's profits are shown below operating profit on the parent company's income statement.

6. Which of the following correctly lists the conditions when the multiples valuation of a subsidiary is appropriate?

   A. The subsidiary is publicly traded, and the parent owns less than 20 percent of the subsidiary.

   B. The subsidiary is not publicly traded, and the parent owns less than 20 percent of the subsidiary.

C. The subsidiary is publicly traded, and the parent owns between 20 percent and 50 percent of the subsidiary.

D. The subsidiary is not publicly traded, and the parent owns between 20 percent and 50 percent of the subsidiary.

7. A corporation has 2 million shares outstanding. Using the following information (all values in millions), calculate the value per share.

   DCF of operations = $320

   Financial subsidiary value = $25

   Employee stock options = $2

   Bonds = $185

   Discontinued operations = $2

   Securitized receivables = $4

   Operating leases = $6

8. Given the following list, put a "+" if it increases a firm's equity value or a "–" if it decreases the firm's value per share of common stock.

Excess real estate	
Preferred stock	
Noncontrolling interest	
Tax loss carryforward	
Unfunded pension liabilities	
Nonconsolidated subsidiaries	

9. Indicate in which cases book value is a reasonable approximation for evaluating the asset or liability. Enter "Yes" if book value is a reasonable approximation and "No" if it is not.

   A. Floating-rate debt: ______

   B. Outstanding bonds that are secure and actively traded: ______

   C. Discontinued operations: ______

   D. Stake in a publicly traded subsidiary: ______

   E. Excess real estate: ______

   F. Loans to nonconsolidated subsidiaries and other companies (assume interest rates and credit risk have not changed): ______

   G. An outstanding convertible bond deep in the money: ______

   H. Employee stock options: ______

10. An analyst is evaluating a corporation's subsidiary by multiplying the value of the stake in the subsidiary when it was acquired times 1 plus

the percentage change in a portfolio of comparable stocks over the same holding period. Based on this information, answer the following questions:

A. What are the conditions when this is a preferred method of valuation for the stake?

B. What is the name of the method?

15

Analyzing the Results

Once the valuation model is complete, an analyst should test its validity, sensitivity to various inputs, and sensitivity to various economic forecasts. A model's validity can be questioned if there are mechanical errors or flaws in economic logic. Understanding how sensitive the valuations are to key inputs and economic conditions gives the analyst a more robust understanding of the long-term value drivers for a firm and the potential for large swings in value.

Verifying valuation results involves checks and balances to see if the model is technically robust by addressing the following relationships: (1) that the balance sheet balances and the correct relationships exist among income, retained earnings, and dividends; (2) that the sum of invested capital plus nonoperating assets equals the cumulative sources of financing; and (3) that the change in excess cash and debt line up with the cash flow statement. A good model will have automatic checks for these relationships.

Checking for economic consistency involves seeing if the results reflect appropriate value driver economics; for example, high growth and return should be reflected in value of operations higher than book value. The analyst should also check to see if the patterns of key financial and operating ratios are consistent with economic logic and, in general, check to see if the results are plausible.

Sensitivity analysis aids in determining the impact of changes of key drivers, and scenario analysis allows for assessing results under a broad set of conditions. Valuation can be very sensitive to small changes in assumptions, which is why market values fluctuate. A good guide is to aim for a valuation range of +/–15 percent, which is similar to the range used by investment bankers.

1. Which of the following is *not* a question related to economic consistency of a model?

   A. Are the patterns intended?

   B. Are the patterns reasonable?

C. Are the patterns chartable?

D. Are the patterns consistent with industry dynamics?

2. To prioritize strategic actions, the analyst should:

A. Take a vote from the major players.

B. Build a sensitivity analysis that tests multiple changes at a time.

C. Follow the priorities of leaders in the industry.

D. Follow Porter's five points.

3. List the criteria for assessing whether a model is technically robust with respect to the following three perspectives.

A. Unadjusted financial statements:____________________

B. Rearranged financial statements:____________________

C. Statement of cash flows:____________________

4. When analyzing scenarios in a scenario analysis, an analyst should review the assumptions of a model with respect to four variables. List and explain those variables.

A. ____________________

B. ____________________

C. ____________________

D. ____________________

5. When making forecasts, increasing one variable usually means decreasing another. List three of the several possible common trade-offs that should be considered in making such forecasts.

A. ____________________

B. ____________________

C. ____________________

6. When using the scenario approach, an analyst should not shortcut the process by deducting the face value of debt from the scenario-weighted value of operations because ____________________.

7. An analyst is estimating the ROIC of a company that has zero fixed costs per unit and pays no taxes. The analyst makes the following forecasts. Sales next year will equal 200 units and will increase at 10 percent for each of the two following years. Prices per unit will be $100, $104, and $110, which simply embody inflation forecasts. Costs per unit will be constant at $90. Current capital invested is $2,000, and the firm will reinvest 50 percent of income.

A. What will be the ROIC for each of the three years?

	Year 1	Year 2	Year 3
Number of units			
Price per unit			
Cost per unit			
Income			
Invested capital			
ROIC			

B. If this is a competitive industry, are the results realistic? Why or why not?

8. The forecasts in Question 7 used several assumptions. Repeat the forecasts where (A) costs increase with inflation, but all other assumptions hold, and (B) sales units remain constant, but all the other assumptions hold (including constant costs).

A.

	Year 1	Year 2	Year 3
Number of units			
Price per unit			
Cost per unit			
Income			
Invested capital			
ROIC			

B.

	Year 1	Year 2	Year 3
Number of units			
Price per unit			
Cost per unit			
Income			
Invested capital			
ROIC			

9. Based on the results in Question 8, assess the sensitivity of your results in Question 7 to each of the relaxed assumptions.

16

Using Multiples

The use of multiples can increase valuations based on DCF analysis. There are five requirements for making useful analyses of comparable multiples: (1) value multibusiness companies as a sum of their parts, (2) use forward estimates of earnings, (3) use the right multiple, (4) adjust the multiple for nonoperating items, and (5) use the right peer group.

Multibusiness companies' various lines of business typically have very different growth and ROIC expectations. Thus, these firms should be valued as a sum of their parts. All multiples should be forward-looking rather than based on historical data, as valuation of firms is based on expectations of future cash flow generation. The right multiple is often the value-to-EBITA ratio:

$$\frac{\text{Value}}{\text{EBITA}} = \frac{(1-T)\left(1-\frac{g}{\text{ROIC}}\right)}{\text{WACC}-g}$$

This measure is superior to the price-to-earnings (P/E) ratio because (1) capital structure affects P/E and (2) nonoperating gains and losses affect earnings. Alternatives to the value-to-EBITA and P/E multiples include the value-to-EBIT ratio, the value-to-EBITDA ratio, the value-to-revenue ratio, the price-to-earnings-growth (PEG) ratio, multiples of invested capital, and multiples of operating metrics. All of these ratios should be adjusted for the effects of nonoperating items. Finally, the peer group is important. The peer group should consist of companies whose underlying characteristics (such as production methodology, distribution channels, and R&D) lead to similar growth and ROIC characteristics.

1. Which two of the following are likely to vary the most among companies within an industry?

   I. Tax rates.

   II. Growth.

III. ROIC.
IV. WACC.
A. I and II.
B. I and III.
C. II and III.
D. III and IV.

2. Which of the following are reasons that the value-to-EBITA ratio is superior to the price-to-earnings ratio as a multiple to aid in valuation?
   I. The P/E is distorted by capital structure.
   II. The P/E is distorted by inflation.
   III. The P/E is distorted by nonoperating gains and losses.
   IV. The P/E is distorted by dividend payouts.
   A. I and III only.
   B. II and III only.
   C. II and IV only.
   D. I, III, and IV only.
3. Comparison of a company's multiples to the arithmetic averages of an industry:
   A. Is one of the more recommended practices, but it may not be the best.
   B. Is the best recommended practice.
   C. Is not recommended.
   D. Is not possible.
4. Increasing growth while holding ROIC, the tax rate, and WACC constant will:
   A. Increase the value-to-EBITA ratio.
   B. Not affect the value-to-EBITA ratio.
   C. Decrease the value-to-EBITA ratio.
   D. Have an undetermined effect on the value-to-EBITA ratio.
5. Given a price-to-earnings (P/E) ratio of 15 and projected earnings growth of 5 percent, what is the PEG ratio? What are the deficiencies of this multiple?
6. Given the following inputs, compute the value-to-EBITA ratio: tax rate = 34 percent, growth rate = 4 percent, ROIC = 10 percent, and WACC = 9 percent.
7. A firm has $600 market value of equity and $300 market value of debt. The firm also has $100 in nonconsolidated subsidiaries and $50 in excess cash. If the firm's expected EBITA is $100, what is the value-to-EBITA ratio?

8. For each of the following characteristics that help determine growth and ROIC, list contrasting types of characteristics to consider when composing appropriate peer groups.

   A. Production methodology: ______________________________

   B. Distribution channels: ______________________________

   C. Research and development: ______________________________

9. Explain why EBITA is superior to:

   A. EBIT: ______________________________

   B. EBITDA: ______________________________

10. Give examples of nonfinancial ratios applied to Internet companies in the 1990s. Comment on their relative usefulness in the valuation of Internet stocks before such stocks matured and the valuation of Internet stocks after the industry matured.

11. When should an analyst use enterprise-to-NOPLAT ratios versus enterprise to EBITA ratios? Explain.

17

Valuing by Parts

Many large companies have multiple business units, each competing in segments with different economic characteristics. Even pure-play companies often have a wide variety of underlying geographical and category segments. If the economics of a company's segments are different, you will generate more insights by valuing each segment and adding them up to estimate the value of the entire company. Trying to value the entire company as a single enterprise will not provide much insight, and your final valuation will likely be noisier than valuing by parts. Consider a simple case where a faster-growing segment has lower returns on capital than a slower-growing segment. If both segments maintain their ROIC, the corporate ROIC would decline as the weights of the different segments change.

Valuing by parts generates better valuation estimates and deeper insights into where and how the company is generating value. That is why it is standard practice in industry-leading companies and among sophisticated investors. Four critical steps for valuing a company by its parts are (1) understanding the mechanics of and insights from valuing a company by the sum of its parts, (2) building financial statements by business unit—based on incomplete information, if necessary, (3) estimating the weighted average cost of capital by business unit, and (4) testing the value based on multiples of peers.

To value a company's individual business units, you need income statements, balance sheets, and cash flow statements. Ideally, these financial statements should approximate what the business units would look like if they were stand-alone companies. Creating financial statements for business units requires consideration of several issues, including (1) allocating corporate overhead costs, (2) dealing with intercompany transactions, (3) understanding financial subsidiaries, and (4) navigating incomplete public information.

1. Which of the following are issues in the creation of the financial statements for business units?

I. Allocating corporate overhead costs.
II. Dealing with intercompany transactions.
III. Estimating unit betas.
IV. Dealing with incomplete information when using public information.

A. I and II only.
B. II and IV only.
C. I, II, and IV only.
D. II, III, and IV only.

2. For multibusiness units, consolidated corporate results:
   A. Must eliminate internal revenues, costs, and profits.
   B. Are not possible.
   C. Are computed by summing the inputs for each accounting entry across units.
   D. Are computed by top-down algorithms that give estimated values based on the economic profit or cost of each entry.
3. Which of the following correctly describes how to determine the beta for a business unit within a multiple-business corporation?
   A. Use the average of the equity betas for the industry.
   B. Use the beta of the multiunit enterprise.
   C. Relever the unlevered sector median beta using the capital structure of the unit.
   D. Relever the unlevered sector median beta using the capital structure of the entire multiple-business corporation.
4. List the steps in valuing a multibusiness company by parts:
   A. ______________________________.
   B. ______________________________.
   C. ______________________________.
   D. ______________________________.
5. List the issues an analyst encounters when creating financial statements for business units:
   A. ______________________________.
   B. ______________________________.
   C. ______________________________.
   D. ______________________________.

6. List three best practices for testing valuation by parts based on multiples of peers:
   A. ______________________________.
   B. ______________________________.
   C. ______________________________.

For questions 7 through 10, answer True or False.

7. CEO salaries should be allocated to business units based on the number of employees in the units.
8. Human resources costs should be allocated to business units based on the number of employees in the units.
9. Financing subsidiaries should be valued separately from other business units.
10. There is undisputed evidence that conglomerate firms trade at a discount relative to a portfolio of pure-play firms.
11. You have estimated the NOPLAT for each of the divisions in a three-division firm at $20 million, $30 million, and $50 million, respectively, for Divisions A, B, and C. Using these figures, you assume that Divisions A, B, and C contribute 20, 30, and 50 percent, respectively, to overall firm value. Is this an appropriate valuation technique? Why or why not?
12. As CFO, you are trying to allocate investment funds across your three-division firm. You observe the revenues last year as $4.0 billion, $3.0 billion, and $3.0 billion, respectively, for Divisions A, B, and C. Using these figures, you assume that Divisions A, B, and C should have investment budgets of 40, 30, and 30 percent, respectively, of the overall firm's investment budget for the year. What might be problematic about this approach?

18

Taxes

In estimating value, an analyst needs to determine the portion of taxes due from the operating activities, then determine the operating cash taxes, and, finally, estimate the value of the corporation recognizing that some taxes are deferred. The available information on the analyzed firm will be incomplete; therefore, analysts can only estimate the operating cash taxes, and the estimates will have errors. Using either the company's statutory tax rate or the company's effective rate with no adjustments is not appropriate for computing operating taxes. One suitable approach is to compute taxes as if the company were financed entirely with equity. To accomplish this task, an analyst could begin with reported taxes and undo financing and nonoperating items one by one. The analyst should make estimates based on the tax rates in the various jurisdictions in which the firm operates.

Estimates of operating taxes actually paid in cash provide a better input for valuation than those estimates that include accruals. As part of the estimation process, the analyst should subtract the increase in net operating deferred tax liabilities (DTLs) from operating taxes. Information for this process should be in the tax footnote. Also, the reorganized balance sheet needs to properly assign deferred tax assets (DTAs) and deferred tax liabilities. For each deferred tax account, there are four valuation methodologies: (1) value the account as part of NOPLAT, (2) value the account as part of a corresponding nonoperating asset or liability, (3) value the account as a separate nonoperating asset, and (4) ignore the account as an accounting convention.

For Questions 1 through 8, answer True or False.

1. With full information, operating taxes can be computed without error.
2. The effects of research and development should be removed from operating taxes.
3. Operating taxes are computed as if the company were financed entirely with equity.

4. It is not correct to use the company's effective tax rate with no adjustments.
5. The income tax footnote is a good source of information for deferred tax liabilities.
6. All deferred tax liabilities are classified as debt.
7. Usually, a company will record a DTL during the year of an acquisition and then draw down the DTL as the intangible amortizes.
8. Making estimates of operating taxes based on tax rates in individual jurisdictions is not recommended.
9. Of the list of deferred tax assets and liabilities (i.e., DTAs and DTLs), indicate whether each is a DTA or a DTL and whether it should be classified as operating or nonoperating.

Account	**DTA or DTL?**	**Operating or nonoperating?**
Nondeductible intangibles		
Tax loss carry-forwards		
Accelerated depreciation		
Pension and postretirement benefits		
Warranty reserves		

10. Complete the table by filling in the blank cells. The ultimate goal is to compute the effective tax rate and the operating tax rate.

	Domestic subsidiary	**Foreign subsidiary**	**R&D tax credits**	**One-time credits**	**Company**
EBITA	3,000	800			
Amortization	(1,000)	(200)			
EBIT					
Interest expense	(800)	(200)			
Gains on asset sales	100	0			
Earnings before taxes					
Taxes			110	88	
Net Income					
Tax rates (percent)					
Statutory rate	30%	40%			
Effective tax rate					
EBITA	3,000	800			

	Domestic subsidiary	Foreign subsidiary	R&D tax credits	One-time credits	Company
Operating taxes			110		
NOPLAT					
Tax rates (percent)					
Statutory rate	30%	40%			
Operating tax rate					

19

Nonoperating Items, Provisions, and Reserves

Strict accounting rules exist for dealing with nonoperating expenses and one-time charges. For determining value, however, these entries and the financial statements require adjustments. Despite popular belief, these entries provide relevant information concerning past performance and future cash flows. A three-step process can aid in assessing the impact of nonoperating charges: (1) reorganize the income statement into operating and nonoperating items, (2) search the notes for embedded one-time items, and (3) analyze each extraordinary item for its impact on future operations.

Noncash expenses usually lower an asset or increase a provision account in the liabilities. In evaluating a business, there are four types of provisions: (1) ongoing operating provisions, (2) long-term operating provisions, (3) nonoperating restructuring provisions, and (4) provisions created to smooth income.

1. Given the following list, indicate if each entry is an item related to the ongoing core business of a company. Enter "Yes" if it relates to the ongoing core business and "No" if it does not.

   A. Litigation-related charges _____

   B. Royalty expense _____

   C. Impairment of goodwill _____

   D. Restructuring charges _____

   E. SG&A expense _____

   F. R&D expense _____

   G. Loss or gain on assets _____

   H. Amortization expense _____

   I. Purchased R&D expense _____

2. Given the following entries concerning revenues and adjustments for provisions for an asset, compute NOPLAT, invested capital, and ROIC on beginning-of-year invested capital. Assume that all invested capital entries are beginning-of-year entries, all revenue entries are for year-end, and year-end equity is $10,000.

   Reserve for income smoothing = $2,500
   Reported EBITA = $4,000
   Increase in income-smoothing reserve = $600
   Reserve for product returns = $800
   Reserve for plant decommissioning = $5,000
   Plant decommissioning reserve accretion = $500
   Provision for restructuring = $400
   Reserve for restructuring = $1,000

3. A firm has just built a plant that it plans to decommission in three years. It estimates the decommissioning costs in three years will be $100 million. The relevant interest rate is 8 percent. Complete the table.

Balance sheet	**Year 1**	**Year 2**	**Year 3**
Starting reserve	0		
Plant-decommissioning expense	30.80		
Interest cost	0		
Decommissioning payout	0	0	(100)
Ending reserve	30.80		0
Income statement			
Reported provision	30.80		

4. Explain the two classifications for acquisition premiums and how in-process R&D fits into the categories.
5. Give an example of when a litigation charge should be considered an operating charge.
6. In computing operating performance, what should the policy be toward goodwill impairments? Why?
7. Explain when the size of a nonoperating expense or one-time charge mentioned in a management discussion and analysis (MD&A) note might determine whether it should be included in the adjustment to NOPLAT. Include the reasoning for the decision.

8. In the following table there is a list of examples of provisions and reserves in column 1 (the far left column). Fill in the blank cells with the appropriate letters.

In column 2, with respect to classification treatment, indicate which of the examples in column 1 is: (A) a nonoperating provision, (B) an income-smoothing provision, (C) an ongoing operating provision, or (D) a long-term operating provision.

In column 3, with respect to treatment in NOPLAT, indicate which of the following corresponds to the examples in column 1: (E) deduct operating portion from revenue to determine NOPLAT and treat interest portion as non-operating, (F) convert accrual provision into cash provision and treat as non-operating, (G) eliminate provision by converting accrual provision into cash provision, or (H) deduct provisions from revenue to determine NOPLAT.

In column 4, with respect to treatment in invested capital, indicate which of the following corresponds to the examples in column 1: (I) deduct reserve from operating assets to determine invested capital, (J) treat reserve as a debt equivalent, (K) (same as J) treat reserve as a debt equivalent, or (L) treat reserve as an equity equivalent.

In column 5, with respect to treatment in valuation, indicate which of the following corresponds to the examples in column 1: (M) provision is part of free cash flow, (N) deduct reserve's present value from the value of operations, (O) not relevant, or (P) deduct reserve's present value from the value of operations.

Examples of provisions and reserves	Classification treatment	Treatment in NOPLAT	Invested capital	Treatment in valuation
Plant decommissioning costs and unfunded retirement plans				
Provisions for the sole purpose of income smoothing				
Product returns and warranties				
Restructuring charges (e.g., expected severance payouts from layoffs)				

20

Leases and Retirement Obligations

Leases, pension obligations, and securitized receivables are like debt obligations, but accounting rules can allow them to be off-balance-sheet items. Such items can bias ROIC upward, which makes competitive benchmarking unreliable; however, valuation may be unaffected.

To adjust for operating leases, the analyst should (1) recognize the lease as both an obligation and asset on the balance sheet (which requires an increase in operating income by adding an implicit interest expense to the income statement and lowering operating expenses by the same amount), (2) adjust WACC for the new leverage ratios, and (3) value the company based on the new free cash flow and WACC. Assuming straight-line depreciation, an estimate of a leased asset's value for the balance sheet is:

$$\text{Asset Value}_{t-1} = \frac{\text{Rental Expense}_t}{\left(k_d + \frac{1}{\text{Life of the Asset}}\right)}$$

Another source of distortion occurs when a company sells a portion of its receivables and thereby reduces accounts receivable on the balance sheet and increases cash flow from operations on the cash flow statement. Despite the favorable changes in accounting measures, the selling of receivables is very similar to increasing debt, because the company pays fees for the arrangement, it reduces its borrowing capacity, and the firm pays higher interest rates on unsecured debt. In the wake of the financial crisis of 2008, accounting policy has tightened. In many cases, securitized receivables are now classified as secured borrowing. In these situations, no adjustment is required. In the infrequent cases where securitized receivables are not capitalized on the balance sheet, the analyst should add back securitized receivables to the balance sheet and make a corresponding increase to short-term debt. These alterations will determine the necessary changes to return on capital, free cash flow, and leverage. Interest expense should increase by the fees paid for securitizing receivables.

Companies must report excess pension assets and unfunded pension obligations on the balance sheet at their current values, but pension accounting can still greatly distort operating profitability. An analyst should take three steps to incorporate excess pension assets and unfunded pension liabilities into enterprise value and the income statement to eliminate accounting distortions. Those three steps are: (1) identify excess pension assets and unfunded liabilities on the balance sheet, (2) add excess pension assets to and deduct unfunded pension liabilities from enterprise value, (3) remove the accounting pension expense from cost of sales and replace it with the service cost and amortization of prior service costs reported in the notes. Much of the necessary information for this process appears in the company's notes.

1. Use the words "lower" or "increase" to fill in the blanks.

   A profitable company has chosen to lease its assets and account for them as operating leases. This move will artificially ____________ operating profits. It will artificially ____________ capital productivity. With respect to return, it is most likely that it will ____________ ROIC.
2. Indicate how an analyst's appropriate adjustments for operating leases should adjust assets, liabilities, and operating income. Fill in each blank with either "lower" or "increase."

   The analyst's adjustments should ____________ assets, ____________ liabilities, and ____________ operating income.
3. Explain the usual relationship of the interest rate used in operating lease adjustments relative to the firm's cost of debt (higher or lower) and why that relationship usually exists.
4. In making adjustments for leases, where or how would an analyst get rental expenses and the value of the leased assets?
5. Using the formula that incorporates the rental expense, asset life, and appropriate interest rate, compute the estimated value of a leased asset at the beginning of an accounting period. The rental expense for the period is $4,000, the cost of debt is 6 percent, and the asset's life is five years.
6. Identify a method for estimating the value of leased assets other than the formula used in Question 5. Does the method tend to overestimate or underestimate the value of the leased assets? Why?
7. Summarize the results of two extensive studies cited in the text (one by Lim, Mann, and Mihov and the other from Ohio State University) concerning how credit agencies adjust for companies that use leases and the power of credit statistics adjusted for operating leases to explain the

interest rates paid by firms that use leases by answering the following questions.

A. What are the effects of using more operating leases on the firm's credit rating and the required yield on new debt?______________________________

B. Can operating leases help explain variations in interest rates? ______________________________

C. What does the overall evidence suggest for how investors, lenders, and rating agencies interpret operating leases? ______________________________

8. Fill in the blanks in the following sentences to indicate how an analyst should adjust for securitized receivables that are not capitalized.

   To determine return on capital, free cash flow, and leverage consistently, make the following adjustments on the balance sheet: ____________________ and ____________________.
   The fees paid for securitizing receivables should be ____________________.

9. Complete the following sentences concerning the adjustments for pensions in valuation.

   Excess pension assets should be treated as ____________, and unfunded pension liabilities should be treated as ____________. With respect to taxes, valuations should be done ____________.

10. Compute the operating profits and operating profits adjusted for pension liabilities and assets, given the following information. The amortized prior-year service cost and the amortization of loss are zero.

    Operating revenues = $1,000

    Operating costs = $600

    Pension interest cost = $700

    Expected return on pension plan assets = $500

    Pension service cost = $150

11. Given the following information, calculate (A) invested capital before the adjustment for leases, (B) the WACC before the adjustment for leases, (C) invested capital after the adjustment for leases, and (D) the WACC after the adjustment for leases.

    Operating assets = $3,000

    Operating liabilities = $1,000

    Book value of debt = $1,500 = Market value of debt

    Book value of equity = $500

Market value of equity = $900

Operating leases = $2,000

After-tax required return on unsecured debt = 6 percent

Required return on equity (CAPM) = 13 percent

After-tax required return on secured debt = 5 percent

A. ______________________________

B. ______________________________

C. ______________________________

D. ______________________________

21

Alternative Measures of Return on Capital

The primary measure of return on capital in the text is return on invested capital (ROIC), defined as net operating profit less adjusted taxes (NOPLAT) divided by invested capital. ROIC correctly reflects return on capital in most cases, but special circumstances require alternative measures. More specifically, investments in intangible assets are expensed, which can introduce a negative bias in ROIC and lead managers to make incorrect decisions concerning how to create value.

This chapter addresses how to handle such complexities, focusing on three issues. First, when does ROIC accurately reflect the true economic return on capital, and when does a more complex measure, such as cash flow return on investment (CFROI) make sense? Second, how should one deal with investments in R&D and marketing and sales that are expensed when they are incurred? Creating pro forma financial statements that capitalize these expenses can provide more insight into the underlying economics of a business. Finally, how should one analyze businesses with very low capital requirements? Here it is recommended to use economic profit, or economic profit scaled by revenues, to measure return on capital.

Investments in R&D and other intangibles should be capitalized for three reasons: (1) to represent historical investment more accurately, (2) to prevent manipulation of short-term earnings, and (3) to improve performance assessments of long-term investments. These change only the perceptions of performance, however, and will not change the value of the firm. Since free cash flow (FCF) includes both operating expenses and investment expenditures, capitalizing an expense will not affect FCF.

The process for capitalizing R&D has three steps: (1) build and amortize the R&D asset using an appropriate asset life, (2) make the appropriate upward adjustment on invested capital, and (3) make the appropriate upward adjustment on NOPLAT. An analyst can apply these adjustments to other expenses, such as an expansion of distribution routes. A couple of drawbacks of making too many such adjustments are the increased ability to manipulate short-term performance and the incentives for managers not to recognize when to write down an asset created from a capitalized expense.

1. Which of the following is *not* in the list of conditions where flow return on investment (CFROI) is a preferable measure to ROIC?

   A. The firm has lumpy investment patterns.

   B. Fixed assets have long lives.

   C. Investments for the firm occur in a regular pattern.

   D. There is a large ratio of fixed assets to working capital.

2. For all but the ________ sector, the difference between CFROI and ROIC estimates is ____.
3. Explain how ROIC with R&D capitalized will compare to R&D expensed over the life of a firm. Which will be higher at different points in the firm's life? Will either or both eventually stabilize? (Hint: See Exhibit 21.9 in the text.)
4. Based on your answer to Question 1, explain why it is so important for an analyst to adjust ROIC when making decisions. (Hint: What are the two drivers of value?)
5. Based on Exhibit 21.10 in the text, how do the ROICs compare when using an estimated asset life of 12 years instead of six years? What are the implications of this comparison for choosing an estimated life of an R&D expense in the capitalization process?
6. Based on Exhibit 21.10, compare the general relationship of ROIC to changing asset life when R&D is 5 percent of revenues and when R&D is 15 percent of revenues. Is the relationship very different? Compute the proportional declines from extending the life from two to four years and from extending it from 10 to 12 years. What are the implications of a comparison of the results?
7. Complete the following table for years 3 and 4 to demonstrate how ROIC adjusted for capitalized R&D will eventually fall below unadjusted ROIC. The assumptions are that growth of revenues is 10 percent each year, production expenses are 50 percent of revenue, R&D is 5 percent of revenue, and investment in physical assets is 20 percent of revenues. Investments are depreciated 10 percent each year. There are no taxes. The difference between unadjusted and adjusted initial capital, 2,000 and 2,180 respectively, reflects capitalized R&D from previous years.

Year	1	2	3	4
Sales	1,000	1,100		
Production expenses	(500)	(550)		
R&D	(50)	(55)		
Depreciation	(200)	(200)		
Operating income	250	295		
Beg of year capital	2,000	2,000		
Investment	(200)	(220)		
ROIC	12.50%			
Adj. beg of year capital	2,180	2,212		
Adj. depreciation	(218)	(221.2)		
Adj. operating income	282	328.8		
Adj. ROIC	12.94%			

8. When comparing the performance of businesses with very different capital intensity and size, using ____________ provides the best insights into performance and value creation.

22

Inflation

Inflation makes analyzing performance and making comparisons difficult. Also, inflation usually impedes the creation of value. Inflation lowers the value of monetary assets, and the firm can rarely pass along the full effects of inflation to customers. Typically, ROIC does not increase enough to compensate the firm for inflation. The increase in inflation from the 1960s to the 1970s was accompanied by a decline in P/E ratios.

During periods of high inflation, the problem becomes much worse. An analyst needs to correct for the following distortions: (1) overstated growth, (2) overestimated capital turnover, (3) overstated operating margins, and (4) distorted credit ratios. When making forecasts in such periods, the analyst can make adjustments in either nominal or real terms, but consistent financial projections require elements of both nominal and real forecasts. Five steps for making forecasts in periods of high inflation are (1) forecast operating performance in real terms, (2) build financial statements in nominal terms, (3) build financial statements in real terms, (4) forecast free cash flow (FCF) in real and nominal terms, and (5) estimate discounted cash flow (DCF) value in real and nominal terms.

1. Given the following list, indicate for which items real or nominal modeling applications are preferred. Put "Real" or "Nominal" in each blank.

   A. EBITA ____________

   B. Sales ____________

   C. Income taxes ____________

   D. EBITDA ____________

   E. Financial statements ____________

   F. Investments in working capital ____________

   G. Capital expenditures ____________

2. Identify three effects of volatile inflation on estimating cash flows.
   A. ______________________________
   B. ______________________________
   C. ______________________________
3. Identify and describe three adjustments to the enterprise DCF and economic profit when attempting to establish the value of a company located in an environment of high inflation.
   A. ______________________________
   B. ______________________________
   C. ______________________________
4. Discuss the limitations of both real and nominal forecasts:
   A. Real forecasts:______________________________
   B. Nominal forecasts:______________________________
5. Identify the five-step approach managers should employ to combine nominal and real forecasts.
   A. ______________________________
   B. ______________________________
   C. ______________________________
   D. ______________________________
   E. ______________________________
6. Given the following information, compute FCF in real terms:

   Real growth is 4 percent, real ROIC is 10 percent, real NOPLAT is \$2,000, real net working capital from the previous year is \$1,000, the inflation index last year was 200, and the inflation index this year is 300.
7. A firm begins with nominal $NWC^N_{t-1} = 100$ and then doubles it to $NWC^N_t = 200$. The price index increases from $IX_{t-1} = 2$ to $IX_t = 2.5$. Based on this information, what is the real investment in NWC in year *t*?
8. Given the following information, compute the real continuing value:

   Real ROIC is 6 percent, real NOPLAT is \$3,000, nominal WACC is 21 percent, inflation is 10 percent, real growth is 4 percent, real net working capital is \$1,500, and real invested capital is \$10,000.
9. Follow the procedures in Exhibit 22.3 in the text to fill in the blanks in the following table and demonstrate that FCF will fall even when the firm increases EBITA at the rate of inflation. Inflation is 20 percent. The firm has a policy of replacing assets at the rate of depreciation, which is 10 percent per year.

	Year 1	Year 2
Sales	2,000	2,320
EBITDA	600	
Depreciation	400	
EBITA	200	
Gross property, plant, and equipment	4,000	
Cumulative depreciation	2,500	2,500
Invested capital	1,500	
EBITDA	600	
Capital expenditures	400	
Free cash flow (FCF)	200	
EBITA growth (percent)	–	
EBITA/sales (percent)		
Return on invested capital (percent)		
FCF growth (percent)	–	

23

Cross-Border Valuation

U.S. Generally Accepted Accounting Principles (GAAP) and International Financial Reporting Standards (IFRS) have been converging over time, and the valuation of companies and subsidiaries in foreign countries has become easier. Yet an analyst needs to consider four issues when analyzing foreign companies: (1) making forecasts in foreign and domestic currencies, (2) estimating the cost of capital in a foreign currency, (3) incorporating foreign-currency risk in valuations, and (4) using translated foreign-currency financial statements.

For a given company, the analyst should forecast the cash flows in the most relevant currency. Then, the analyst should use either the spot-rate method or the forward-rate method to convert the value of the cash flows into that of the parent company. It is important to use consistent monetary assumptions in the process (e.g., concerning inflation and interest rates). When estimating the cost of capital, the analyst should use the equity premium from a global portfolio without an adjustment for currency risk. When translating statements into another currency, there are three choices: the current method, the temporal method, and the inflation-adjusted current method. Usually, the current method is the most appropriate approach.

1. Identify the currency translation method to use in treating a foreign subsidiary in each of the following cases.
   A. The analyst is using U.S. GAAP, and the country of the subsidiary is experiencing hyperinflation.
   B. The analyst is using IFRS, and the country of the subsidiary is experiencing moderate inflation.
   C. The analyst is using U.S. GAAP, and the country of the subsidiary is experiencing moderate inflation.
   D. The analyst is using IFRS, and the country of the subsidiary is experiencing hyperinflation.

2. Describe the forward-rate method for evaluating a foreign subsidiary and explain why the forward-rate method is more complex than the spot-rate method in estimating the value. Include in the discussion the steps needed to remedy possible problems.
3. List and summarize the three categories of assumptions needed when making projections of and discounting cash flows in different currencies.

   A. ______________________________

   B. ______________________________

   C. ______________________________
4. Summarize the main point of Exhibit 23.4 in the text.
5. Complete the table using the procedures in Exhibit 23.1 in the text. One value has been provided in most rows to help you get started in the process.

Monetary Data for Computing the Present Value of a Norwegian Subsidiary of an American Corporation

	Year 1	Year 2	Year 3	Year 4	Year 5	Year 6
Foreign currency (Norwegian kroner—NOK)						
Cash flows						
Nominal cash flow	300	320	340	365	395	440
Real cash flow	297					
Inflation (percent)	1.00	2.00	2.00	3.00	3.00	3.00
Interest rates (percent)						
Real interest rate	2.00	2.00	2.00	2.00	2.00	2.00
Nominal forward interest rate				5.06		
Nominal interest yield						4.38
Spot exchange rate NOK/USD	5					
Forward exchange rate					4.62	
Domestic currency (U.S. dollars—USD)						
Interest rates						
Nominal interest yield				5.57		
Nominal forward interest rate		5.06				
Real interest rate	3.00	3.00	3.00	3.00	3.00	3.00
Inflation (percent)	2.00	2.00	3.00	3.00	4.00	4.00
Cash flows						
Real cash flow					82.13	
Nominal cash flow		65.91				

6. Using the information from Question 5, fill in the table and compute the present value of the cash flows in dollars using the spot-rate method and the forward-rate method.

Discounted Cash Flows and Present Value of Subsidiary

NOK discount rate
PV of NOK cash flows
Sum of PV of NOK cash flows
PV of NOK CFs × Spot rate
USD discount rate
PV of NOK CFs × Forward rates
Sum of PV of USD cash flows

24

Case Study: Heineken

Analyzing a company's future performance and estimating its value begin with examining historical and current data and then making projections. An analyst should make several sets of forecasts or scenarios using different assumptions concerning the business environment and the strategy of the firm. A simple example is where an analyst creates only two or three scenarios (e.g., a business-as-usual scenario, an aggressive marketing or acquisition scenario, and an operational improvement scenario).

The analyst should estimate value using various explicit forecast horizons and different methods. Recall from earlier chapters that there are usually two periods to forecast: the explicit forecast period and the period after that in which the challenge is to estimate the continuing value for that period. There is also the choice of using the free cash flow (FCF) method and the economic-profit method for estimating value. The analyst should use both methods and compare the results. By estimating value using different explicit forecast horizons and methods, the analyst can verify that the model is robust and that the assumptions are consistent.

1. Given the following historical data and assumptions, forecast Saws and Drills Corporation's FCF for the conservative scenario in the first template (A) and the aggressive scenario in the second template (B). Use beginning of year invested capital for ROIC calculations.

	2010	2011	2012	2013	2014
Current assets	499	489	443	429	484
Current liabilities	240	236	255	237	369
Debt in current liabilities	25	12	7	21	78
Long-term debt	218	200	244	207	236
Total assets	686	693	598	579	730

	2010	2011	2012	2013	2014
Capital expenditures	34	34	16	18	23
Change in deferred taxes	4	(5)	3	2	2
Sales	851	838	754	789	1,029
Operating expenses	626	624	579	592	765
SG&A expenses	151	157	132	134	191
Depreciation	23	24	24	21	26
Investment income	4	2	2	3	2
Interest expense	22	20	19	19	16
Miscellaneous income, net	3	(33)	(75)	–	(70)
Income taxes	18	4	10	11	8

A. Conservative: Saws and Drills Corporation is barely able to hold its own in the global arena of faster-paced technological change and customer demands.

Goal: Maintain historical sales, operating, and general expense structures: operating expense/sales of 75 percent, SG&A/sales of 18.6 percent, taxes of 40 percent, working capital/sales of 18.75 percent, net fixed assets/sales of 24 percent, and three years of sales growth at 20 percent per year.

	Historic		Forecast	
Conservative	**2014**	**2015**	**2016**	**2017**
Working capital				
Net fixed assets				
Invested capital				
Net investment				
Debt				
Equity				
Sales growth		20.00%	20.00%	20.00%
Net sales	1,029.00			
Operating expense				
SG&A				
Depreciation				
Operating income				
Taxes on EBIT				

Conservative	Historic 2014	Forecast 2015	2016	2017
Change in deferred tax				
NOPLAT				
ROIC				
Debt/invested capital		65.00%	65.00%	65.00%
Equity/invested capital				
Tax rate		40.00%	40.00%	40.00%
Interest rate		6.00%	7.00%	7.00%
Growth (investment/capital)				
Investment rate (growth/ROIC)				
EBIT/sales				
Sales/invested capital				
Working capital/sales		18.750%	18.750%	18.750%
NFA/sales				
Operating expense/sales		75.000%	75.000%	75.000%
SG&A/sales		18.600%	18.600%	18.600%
Depreciation/sales		2.527%	2.527%	2.527%
Change in deferred tax/sales		0.194%	0.194%	0.194%
Free cash flow				

B. Aggressive: Saws and Drills Corporation introduces significant changes and increases to its product line and ability to meet technological change in the industry.

Goal: Improve all expense structures at high levels of sales growth over the near term; operating expense/sales of 74 percent, 73 percent, 73 percent for three years; SG&A/sales of 16 percent; depreciation/sales of 2.5 percent; taxes of 40 percent; working capital/sales of 18.75 percent; net fixed assets/sales of 24 percent; and three years of sales growth of 40 percent per year.

Aggressive	Historic 2014	Forecast 2015	2016	2017
Working capital				
Net fixed assets				
Invested capital				

Aggressive	Historic	Forecast		
Aggressive	2014	2015	2016	2017
Net investment				
Debt				
Equity				
Sales growth		40.00%	40.00%	40.00%
Net sales	1,029.000			
Operating expense				
SG&A				
Depreciation				
Operating income				
Taxes on EBIT				
Change in deferred tax				
NOPLAT				
ROIC				
Debt/invested capital		65.00%	65.00%	65.00%
Equity/invested capital				
Tax rate		40.00%	40.00%	40.00%
Interest rate		6.00%	7.00%	7.00%
Growth (investment/capital)				
Investment rate (growth/ROIC)				
EBIT/sales				
Sales/invested capital				
Working capital/sales		18.750%	18.750%	18.750%
NFA/sales				
Operating expense/sales		74.000%	73.000%	73.000%
SG&A/sales		16.000%	16.000%	16.000%
Depreciation/sales		2.500%	2.500%	2.500%
Change in deferred tax/sales		0.194%	0.194%	0.194%
Free cash flow				

2. Demonstrate how choosing different explicit forecast horizons can give the same estimate of value. To do this, fill in the following tables where the first template has a two-year explicit forecast horizon and the second template has a five-year explicit forecast horizon. The RONIC is 15 percent, the growth rate is 6 percent, the operating tax rate is 25 percent, and the WACC is 10 percent.

A.

$ million	Today	Year 1	Year 2	Year 3 (for CV)
Revenues	300.0	318.0	337.1	357.3
Operating costs	(270.0)	(286.2)	(303.4)	(321.6)
Operating margin	30.0	31.8	33.7	35.7
Operating taxes	–			
NOPLAT	–			
Net investment	–	(9.5)	(10.1)	**CV**
Free cash flow	–			
Discounted cash flow				
Discount factor	–			
Discounted cash flow	–			
Value of operations				
	$ million	**% of total**		
Discounted cash flow				
Present value of CV				
Value of operations				

B.

$ million	Today	Year 1	Year 2	Year 3	Year 4	Year 5	Year 6 (for CV)
Revenues	300.0	318.0	337.1	357.3	378.7	401.5	425.6
Operating costs	(270.0)	(286.2)	(303.4)	(321.6)	(340.9)	(361.3)	(383.0)
Operating margin	30.0	31.8	33.7	35.7	37.9	40.1	42.6
Operating taxes	–						
NOPLAT	–						
Net investment	–	(9.5)	(10.1)	(10.7)	(11.4)	(12.0)	**CV**
Free cash flow	–						478.8
Discounted cash flow							
Discount factor	–						
Discounted cash flow	–						
Value of operations							
	$ million	**% of total**					
Discounted cash flow							
Present value of CV							
Value of operations							

C. Compare your computed value for both time horizons. Provide an explanation of your results.

3. Fill in the following template to demonstrate the equivalence between free cash flow and economic profit (EP) estimates of value with a model similar to the five-year horizon model in Question 2, part (B).

$ million	**Today**	**Year 1**	**Year 2**	**Year 3**	**Year 4**	**Year 5**	**Year 6 (for CV)**
Revenues	300.0	318.0	337.1	357.3	378.7	401.5	425.6
Operating costs	(270.0)	(286.2)	(303.4)	(321.6)	(340.9)	(361.3)	(383.0)
Operating margin	30.0	31.8	33.7	35.7	37.9	40.1	42.6
Operating taxes	–						
NOPLAT	–						
Invested capital$_{t-1}$	–	159.0	168.5	178.7	189.4	200.7	212.8
∗ Cost of capital	–	10.0%	10.0%	10.0%	10.0%	10.0%	10.0%
Capital charge	–						
Economic profit	–						
Discounted economic profit							
Economic profit	–						
Discount factor	–						
Discounted economic profit	–						
Value of operations	**$ million**	**% of total**					
Invested capital	159.0	44.4%					
PV(economic profit)	33.6	9.4%					
PV(continuing value)	165.1	46.2%					
Value of operations	357.8	100.0%					

25

Corporate Portfolio Strategy

Each firm should manage its portfolio of businesses by determining whether it is the best owner of each business in the portfolio (i.e., whether it can create the most value from each business it owns). If so, then the firm should keep the business. If not, the firm should divest the business for a value that exceeds its value to the firm. It should use the same basic philosophy when considering adding businesses to the portfolio.

Firms that can add the most value to a business usually have one of five advantages: (1) unique links with other businesses within the firm, (2) distinctive skills, (3) better governance, (4) better insight and foresight, and (5) an influence on critical stakeholders. The firm that can offer one or more of these advantages can change over time as the firm, business, or economy changes. At the beginning of a business, for example, the founders are the best managers, but this will usually change. The needs of the business change as it expands and needs additional capital, a wider variety of management skills, and more connections to other businesses such as buyers and suppliers. A typical path of a business begins with the founders and ends in a conglomerate corporation.

When constructing a portfolio of businesses, the firm should take five steps: (1) assess the gap between a firm's current value and its as-is value, (2) identify internal opportunities to improve operations, (3) determine if some businesses in the firm should be divested, (4) identify potential acquisitions or other initiatives to create new growth, and (5) assess if the company's value can increase from changes in capital structure. Diversification considerations are not part of the list. The purported benefits of diversification are illusive, while the costs are real. For instance, diversification can hurt the value of the firm if it lowers the ability of the managers to focus on how to create value for each of the various businesses.

1. List and explain the five main reasons a given firm might be the best owner of a business.
   A. ______________________________
   B. ______________________________
   C. ______________________________
   D. ______________________________
   E. ______________________________
2. From the list of potential owners, choose which is most likely to be the best owner given the indicated need in the list that follows. Put the appropriate letter in the blank. Some are used more than once. In most cases, there is one best answer, but others might apply.
   A. Private equity.
   B. Founders.
   C. Conglomerate.
   D. Venture capital.
      i. Managerial experience: ______________________________
      ii. Distribution channels: ______________________________
      iii. Additional funds: ______________________________
      iv. Dynamic decision making: ______________________________
      v. Innovation: ______________________________
      vi. Supplier network: ______________________________
      vii. Recapitalization: ______________________________
3. Given the list to the right, match each activity to its corresponding level in the five-step value-adding process from first to last on the left. One activity does not belong on the list.

i. ________	A. Consider a trade sale of a business.
ii. ________	B. Determine the optimal capital structure.
iii. ________	C. Determine diversification effects.
iv. ________	D. Assess the gaps between the valuations of owners and managers.
v. ________	E. Identify growth initiatives.
	F. Identify possible improvements of margins and efficiency.

4. Read the case and then answer the questions that follow.

   Conglom Corporation owns three businesses: CleanUp, Ennerall, and Corwin Company. CleanUp makes and distributes soap and shampoo. Ennerall developed a new vitamin-rich energy drink three years ago with a newly discovered extract from a jungle herb. The sales of the drink rose dramatically when it was first introduced to the market. Corwin Company makes razor blades. CleanUp is the core business of Conglom Corporation and generates 70 percent of the discounted cash flows. It has a low cost of capital, and its ROIC is above the cost of capital. It acquired Ennerall when its contacts in the convenience store industry got samples of Ennerall's product, which quickly sold. After two years of quick growth via CleanUp's drugstore connections, the uniqueness of Ennerall's product has worn off, and sales have leveled off. The managers of Ennerall have been investing large sums attempting to develop new variations of their product that they hope will steal market share from their rivals. Corwin Company was a family business that had lost a lot of value due to the heirs of the founders neglecting the business and not monitoring the managers. Conglom bought the Corwin Company because the price was attractive, and the sales and marketing team of CleanUp helped increase the value of the Corwin Company to the point where its returns and growth are on par with CleanUp's.

A. In the case of Ennerall and Corwin Company, indicate what likely made Conglom the best owner in each case. Mention at least one of the five reasons a given firm might be the best owner as listed in the text.
   Ennerall: ______________________________
   Corwin Company: ______________________________
B. Should Conglom divest either Ennerall or Corwin Company? Why?

26

Performance Management

Performance management systems align decisions with short- and long-term objectives and the overall strategy. Such systems typically include long-term strategic plans, short-term budgets, capital budgeting systems, performance reporting and reviews, and compensation frameworks. The rigor and honesty of implementing the system is at least as important as the system itself. Implementing the system includes choosing the metrics, composing the scorecard, and setting the meeting calendars.

Choosing the right metrics means identifying the value drivers. Typically, the ultimate drivers are long-term growth, ROIC, and the cost of capital. Short-, medium-, and long-term value drivers determine growth, ROIC, and the cost of capital. Short-term value drivers are usually the easiest to quantify, and examples include sales productivity, operating cost productivity, and capital productivity. Medium-term value drivers consist of measures of commercial health, cost structure health, and asset health. Long-term value drivers address strategic issues such as ways to exploit new growth areas and the existence of potential market threats. Understanding the value drivers allows the managers to have a common language for their goals and to make better choices of trade-offs between critical and less critical drivers.

Managers should follow some of the guidelines of the balanced scorecard approach, introduced by Robert S. Kaplan and David P. Norton in "The Balanced Scorecard: Measures That Drive Performance" (*Harvard Business Review*, February 1992), which can reflect many aspects of the firm and its goals. However, the choice of critical drivers should be tailored to the firm's businesses. For example, in contrast to the balanced scorecard approach, a tree based on profit-and-loss structure is often the most natural and easiest to complete. The targets need to be challenging and realistic, however, and should not consist of only a single point. One recommendation is the use of base and stretch targets, where achieving the latter reaps a reward for the manager and not a penalty.

In addition to determining drivers and targets, managers should assess organizational health, which is determined by the people, skills, and culture of the company. Managers should help set the targets to better understand these issues. Fact-based reviews with appropriate rewards should depend on (1) stock performance where macroeconomic and industry trends have been removed, (2) long-term assessments that might mean deferring rewards, and (3) measures of performance against both quantitative and qualitative drivers. The firm should harness the power of nonfinancial incentives, such as creating a culture that attracts and motivates quality employees.

1. Assessing the ability to exploit new growth areas and potential new threats is the focus of:

   A. Short-term value drivers.

   B. Medium-term value drivers.

   C. Long-term value drivers.

   D. None of these.

2. Which of the following are components of a good planning and performance management system?

   I. Promoting a common language of goals and performance.

   II. Including metrics, corporate meeting calendars, and scorecards.

   III. Promoting an understanding of value drivers.

   IV. Having honesty and rigor in implementation.

   A. I, II, and III only.

   B. I, III, and IV only.

   C. II, III, and IV only.

   D. I, II, III, and IV.

3. Which of the following are true of the balanced scorecard method introduced by Kaplan and Norton (1992)?

   I. It posits that there are more measures of performance than just financial performance.

   II. It is used by both for-profit and nonprofit organizations.

   III. It advocates that companies choose their own set of metrics for the outermost branches of the value creation tree.

   IV. Customer satisfaction and learning are as important as long-term value creation.

   A. I and II only.

   B. I, II, and III only.

   C. I, II, and IV only.

   D. II, III, and IV only.

4. What is the role of the operating managers in setting the targets and in reading the measures they are targeting?
   A. None.
   B. Operating managers should set targets but should not be involved in reading the measures.
   C. Operating managers should be involved in reading the measures but not in setting the targets.
   D. Operating managers should be involved in both setting the targets and reading the measures.
5. The recommendation concerning stock-based compensation is:
   A. Not to use it at all.
   B. That it has been proven to be the best method to motivate managers because markets are efficient.
   C. It is useful, but macroeconomic and industry effects should be removed in formulating the compensation.
   D. It should be used sporadically depending on the conditions of the market.
6. Commercial health metrics indicate whether the company can do what with its current revenue growth?
7. What is one key issue concerning accurately assessing a company's recent strong growth relative to long-term growth?
8. A well-defined and appropriately selected set of key value drivers ought to allow management to do what?
9. A diagnostic check of organizational health would typically measure what four aspects of the firm?
   A. ____________________
   B. ____________________
   C. ____________________
   D. ____________________
10. Indicate whether each of the following value drivers is a short-term driver, a medium-term driver, or a long-term driver.
    A. Asset health: ____________________
    B. Operating cost productivity: ____________________
    C. Cost structure health: ____________________
    D. Strategic health: ____________________
    E. Sales productivity: ____________________
    F. Capital productivity: ____________________
    G. Commercial health: ____________________

11. Explain an alternative to a single-point performance target that uses two points of reference, how those points are determined, and how managers should be motivated with respect to them.

27

Mergers and Acquisitions

Acquisitions rarely create value unless they do one or more of the following: (1) improve performance of the target company, (2) remove excess capacity, (3) create market access for the acquirer's or target's products, (4) acquire skills or technologies at a lower cost and/or more quickly than could be done without the acquisition, (5) exploit a business's industry-specific scalability, and (6) pick winners early. Most of the value of an acquisition goes to the target's shareholders unless one or more of the following hold for the acquirer: (1) it had strong performance before the acquisition, (2) it can pay a low premium, (3) it had fewer competitors in the bidding process, and (4) the acquired assets were from a private firm or a subsidiary of a large company. The value created for the acquirer is:

$$\begin{aligned}\text{Value Created for Acquirer} = {} & (\text{Stand} - \text{Alone Value of Target} \\ & + \text{Value of Performance Improvements}) \\ & - (\text{Market Value of Target} \\ & + \text{Acquisition Premium})\end{aligned}$$

Empirical research has shown that acquisitions have come in waves and generally rose when stock prices were high, interest rates were low, and one or more large deals had already taken place. Also, only about a third of the deals created value for the acquirer, a third destroyed value, and the remaining third had unclear results.

Cost savings can create value, but estimating those savings requires a framework. As an example for a generic firm, the analyst might allocate the savings into six categories: R&D, procurement, manufacturing, sales and marketing, distribution, and administration. Assumed cost savings should be estimated and categorized in detail to avoid double counting. It is recommended that those directly involved in the cost-savings process be involved in the estimations of cost savings.

Revenue analysis has both explicit and implicit considerations. Revenue improvements generally have four sources: (1) increasing sales to a higher peak level, (2) reaching a peak level faster, (3) extending the life of products, and (4) adding new products. Revenue could increase from higher prices, but antitrust regulation can prevent higher prices unless the quality of the products increases.

Generally, an acquiring firm's stockholders benefit more if the firm uses stock instead of cash for the acquisition. Although the stock offering can lead to dilution, it lowers the risk to the acquirer and allocates more risk to the target firm's shareholders. Research has shown that stock prices react to creation of intrinsic value in an acquisition and that dilution and other accounting issues do not matter.

1. Which of the following correctly summarizes the approximate proportion of acquisitions that create or destroy value for the acquiring company's shareholders?

   A. Approximately 20 percent create value, 20 percent destroy value, and for the remaining it is not clear.

   B. Approximately $33\frac{1}{3}$ percent create value, $33\frac{1}{3}$ percent destroy value, and for the remaining it is not clear.

   C. Approximately 50 percent create value, 20 percent destroy value, and for the remaining it is not clear.

   D. Approximately 66 percent create value, 17 percent destroy value, and for the remaining it is not clear.

2. Which of the following has been found to be a predictor concerning whether an acquiring firm's shareholders will benefit from an acquisition?

   A. The size of the target.

   B. The P/E of the acquirer is higher than that of the target before the acquisition.

   C. The target and the acquirer are in the same industry.

   D. The acquirer had strong earnings and price growth for several years before the acquisition.

3. The analysis of cost savings should include an industry-specific business system. Which of the following is *not* one of the three criteria that an insightful business system will fulfill?

   A. Uses a top-down approach.

   B. Assigns each cost item of the target to one segment of the business system.

   C. Uses detail to identify the precise source of the savings.

   D. Assigns the savings within the bidder's organization in the appropriate segments in the business system.

4. Which of the following are true concerning the capturing of synergies from an acquisition?

I. Improvements generally come over the long run and do not appear until after the first year.
II. Explicit costs to consider are the cost of decommissioning plants and severance pay.
III. Acquirers often underestimate benefits and do not capture all available synergies.
IV. Implicit costs include rebranding campaigns and the cost of integrating technologies.

A. I and II only.
B. I and IV only.
C. I, II, and III only.
D. II and IV only.

5. When an acquiring firm is making the decision whether to offer cash or stock for a target, it should be more inclined to offer cash if:

I. The stock market is in a bubble.
II. There is a higher level of confidence in the acquisition creating value.
III. The acquiring firm has relatively low debt-to-equity ratios.
IV. The target is larger.

A. I and II only.
B. I and IV only.
C. II and III only.
D. III and IV only.

6. Which of the following is most accurate concerning the findings of the study of 90 acquisitions by McKinsey's Merger and Management practice?

A. Managers were better able to realize estimated cost savings than estimated revenue increases.
B. Managers were better able to realize estimated revenue increases than estimated cost savings.
C. Managers were able to realize estimated cost savings and estimated revenue increases fairly well and about equally well.
D. Managers were not able to realize estimated cost savings nor estimated revenue increases with any success.

7. With respect to the wavelike behavior of acquisitions, list the three market conditions that have led to a rise in the number of acquisitions.

A. ______________________________
B. ______________________________
C. ______________________________

8. In the following list, identify whether the indicated activity is one of the archetypical strategies that has a higher probability of creating value or one of the more difficult strategies for creating value. Write "Archetypical" or "Difficult" in the blanks.
   A. Accelerating market access for target's or buyer's products: ________________
   B. Picking winners early and helping them develop their business: ________________
   C. Consolidating to improve competitive behavior: ________________
   D. Consolidating to remove excess capacity from industry: ________________
   E. Using a roll-up strategy: ________________
   F. Improving the target company's performance: ________________
   G. Entering into a transformational merger: ________________
   H. Buying cheap: ________________
   I. Getting skills or technologies faster or at a lower cost: ________________
9. A firm is considering making an acquisition with either borrowed cash or issued stock. With the cash acquisition, the earnings per share (EPS) after the acquisition will increase 20 percent. The stock acquisition will increase EPS only 10 percent. Even so, explain why the purchase with cash can destroy more value or create less value than the purchase with stock.
10. With reference to Question 9, what is the general implication concerning the importance of accounting measures in assessing the possible benefits and the appropriate strategy for an acquisition?
11. Exhibit 27.7 in the text presents a list of cost-saving categories by function for a generic firm. List the six functions and give at least two examples for each function.

Function	Examples
1	i ii
2	i ii
3	i ii
4	i ii

Function	Examples
5	i
	ii
6	i
	ii

12. An all-equity firm worth $100 billion acquires for $8 billion cash a firm whose postacquisition value will be $10 billion. The acquiring firm had the cash and did not need to borrow. The current market value of the target is $6 billion. What is the estimated return to the shareholders of the acquiring firm and to the shareholders of the target firm?

28

Divestitures

Managers should devote as much time to divestitures as they do to acquisitions; however, managers tend to delay divesting, which leads to the loss of potential value creation. Divestments can create value both around the time of the announcement and in the long term. A divestiture creates value because of the "best owner" principle whereby the old owner's culture or expertise is not well suited for the needs of the divested business. A mature parent company divesting an innovative growth division is the typical example; however, companies ripe for divestiture could be at any stage in their life cycle.

Considerations in divesting are (1) possible losses from synergies and shared assets and systems; (2) disentanglement costs, such as legal and advisory fees and fiscal changes; (3) stranded costs; (4) legal, contractual, and regulatory barriers; and (5) the pricing and liquidity of assets. The costs from synergy losses, for example, may be subtle, and existing contracts may have to be renegotiated. Evidence shows that the level of liquidity of the divested assets plays a role in the amount of value created.

Divestitures can be private transactions, such as trade sales and joint ventures, or they can be public transactions. Private transactions generally lead to more value creation for the seller. Public transactions include IPOs, carve-outs, spin-offs (demergers), split-offs, and the issuance of a tracking stock. Public transactions can be beneficial over the long term if the industry is consolidating. Several types of public transactions often generate negative returns, however, and the divestiture is usually temporary. In the case of carve-outs, for example, the market-adjusted long-term performance for carve-out parents and subsidiaries is usually negative, and usually minority carve-outs are eventually fully sold or reacquired.

For Questions 1 through 9, answer True or False.

1. Both divestitures and acquisitions occur in waves.
2. Managers devote as much time to divestitures as they do to acquisitions.

3. Companies that employ a balanced portfolio approach to acquisitions and divestures have outperformed companies that rarely divest.
4. The liquidity of the assets of the divested company plays a role in the amount of value created.
5. Combining various businesses with different operating risk profiles may result in a group with a higher relative debt capacity than some of the businesses individually are able to sustain.
6. After most divestments, at least initially, the parent company maintains control over the business unit.
7. The possibility of a negative effect on earnings per share or price-to-earnings ratio (P/E) appears to play a role in managers' willingness to divest.
8. A profitable, cash-generating business and a high-growth business can be candidates for divestiture.
9. Tracking stocks are more popular than carve-outs and spin-offs because they do a better job of delivering the benefits sought by managers.
10. Which of the following is *not* true concerning spin-offs?
    A. Overall, they have not created value for the parent companies.
    B. Overall, they have created value for the spin-offs.
    C. The parent company gives up control of the subsidiary.
    D. Whether or not the spin-off is a focus-improving strategy is important with respect to value creation.
11. According to Exhibit 28.5 in the text, which of the following trajectories had a positive median market-adjusted return?
    I. Those that eventually became independent.
    II. Those that eventually merged with or were acquired by other companies.
    III. Those that were reacquired by the parent.
    IV. Those that were delisted.
       A. I only.
       B. I and III only.
       C. II and III only.
       D. I, II, III, and IV.
12. When a parent company is planning to divest and is making a choice between a public and a private transaction, if the goal is to capture value more quickly, which is usually the better choice?
    A. A public transaction.
    B. A private transaction.

C. Neither has a good record of capturing value quickly.

D. Neither, because each captures value about as quickly as the other.

13. Which of the following is most accurate concerning the losses and impediments caused by legal, contractual, or regulatory barriers in the divestment process?

A. They can greatly distort the value creation and seriously slow down the process.

B. They do not greatly distort the value creation, but they do seriously slow down the process.

C. They can greatly distort the value creation, but generally do not slow down the process.

D. They neither distort the value creation nor seriously slow down the process.

14. Which of the following is *not* true concerning tracking stocks?

A. They create a separate class of parent shares.

B. They are distributed to existing parent shareholders.

C. It is a way to keep the liabilities of the parent and subsidiary separate.

D. The parent company maintains control of the subsidiary.

15. For each type of divestiture, indicate if it is a public or private divestiture and select the letter associated with the closest definition from the list following the table. One definition does not belong on the list.

Type of divestiture	Public or private?	Definition (letter from list)
Trade sale		
Spin-off		
Split-off		
Carve-out		
IPO		
Joint venture		

A. A combination of part or all of a business with other industry players, other companies in the value chain, or venture capitalists.

B. Sale of part of the shares in a subsidiary to new shareholders in the stock market.

C. Distribution of all shares in a subsidiary to existing shareholders of the parent company.

D. Sale of part or all of a business to a strategic or financial investor.

E. Government outright purchase of subsidiary by eminent domain.

F. Sale of all shares of a subsidiary to new shareholders in the stock market.
G. An offer to existing shareholders of the parent company to exchange their shares for shares in the subsidiary.

29

Capital Structure, Dividends, and Share Repurchases

Managers should manage capital structure with the goal of not destroying value as opposed to trying to create value. There is usually more to lose than to gain when making a decision in this area. There are three components of a company's financial decisions: (1) how much to invest, (2) how much debt to have, and (3) how much cash to return to shareholders. Managers have many choices concerning capital structure (e.g., using equity, straight debt, convertibles, and off-balance-sheet financing). Managers can create value from using tools other than equity and straight debt under only a few conditions. Even when using more exotic forms of financing like convertibles and preferred stock, fundamentally it is a choice between debt and equity.

Managers must recognize the many trade-offs to both the firm and investors when choosing between debt and equity financing. The firm increases risk but saves on taxes by using debt; however, investing in debt rather than equity probably increases the tax liability to investors. Debt has been shown to impose a discipline on managers and discourage overinvestment, but it can also lead to business erosion and bankruptcy. Higher debt increases the conflicts among the stakeholders. Most companies choose a capital structure that gives them a credit rating between BBB– and A+, which indicates these are effective ratings, and capital structure does not have a large effect on value in most cases. It is true, however, that capital structure can make a difference for companies at the far end of the coverage spectrum.

Credit ratings are a useful summary indicator of capital structure health and are a means of communicating information to shareholders. The two main determinants of credit ratings are size and interest coverage. Two important coverage ratios are the EBITA-to-interest ratio and the debt-to-EBITA ratio.

The former is a short-term measure, and the latter is more useful for long-term planning.

Managers must weigh the benefits of managing capital structure against the costs of the choices and the possible signals the choices send to investors. Methods to manage capital structure include changing the dividends, issuing and buying back equity, and issuing and paying off debt. When designing a long-term capital structure, the firm should project surpluses and deficits, develop a target capital structure, and decide on tactical measures. The tactical, short-term tools include changing the dividend, repurchasing shares, and paying an extraordinary dividend.

1. Indicate whether the following situations are more likely to result from a higher or a lower level of leverage. Fill in the blank with "Higher" if the outcome is the result of higher leverage and "Lower" if it is the result of lower leverage.
   A. Business erosion: ______________
   B. Increased investor conflicts: ______________
   C. Corporate overinvestment: ______________
   D. Bankruptcy: ______________
   E. Tax savings for the firm: ______________
   F. Tax savings for the investors: ______________
   G. Focusing on growth instead of value: ______________
   H. Shareholders preferring higher-risk projects: ______________
2. List the order of financing choices according to the pecking-order theory.
   A. First choice: ______________________________
   B. Second choice: ______________________________
   C. Third choice: ______________________________

   Explain the evidence for or against the pecking-order theory.

3. Using the information in Exhibit 29.4 in the text, rank the following from highest to lowest in terms of the proportion of firms with market capitalization greater than $5 billion with these specific ratings: BB, A, BBB, AA.

   ______________________________ (highest)

   ____

   ____

   ______________________________ (lowest)

4. Using the information in Exhibit 29.4 in the text, rank the following from highest to lowest in terms of the proportion of firms with market capitalization greater than $1 billion with these specific ratings: BB, A, BBB, AA.

   ______________________________ (highest)

   ____

   ____

   ______________________________ (lowest)

5. Rank the following, from highest to lowest, with respect to their importance in determining credit ratings.

   A. Size.

   B. Use of a complex capital structure.

   C. Coverage.

6. What is the market-based ratings approach? Why might it be superior to using ratings to assess a firm's creditworthiness?

7. Indicate whether each of the following generally has a positive or a negative effect on share price. Put a "+" or "–" in each blank.

   A. Dividend increase: __

   B. Issuing debt: __

   C. Issuing equity: __

   D. Extraordinary dividend: __

   E. Share repurchase: __

   F. Dividend decrease: __

   G. Debt repayment: __

   H. Initiating dividend payments: __

8. List the three conditions that justify a nonfinancial firm's use of derivatives to hedge risk.

   A. ______________________________

   B. ______________________________

   C. ______________________________

9. Explain the conditions under which it would make sense for a firm to issue convertible debt. Explain why high-growth companies tend to use convertible debt more than other companies.

   A. Convertible debt makes sense when:

   ____

   ____

   ____

B. High-growth companies tend to use more convertible debt because:

A. ______

B. ______

C. ______

10. List two reasons why enterprise value initially increases as leverage increases from zero:

A. ______

B. ______

List two reasons that enterprise value decreases as leverage increases beyond a certain point:

A. ______

B. ______

11. Explain why well-managed and profitable companies appear to undervalue the benefits associated with an optimal capital structure.

30

Investor Communications

Managers should communicate with investors to help align the value of the stock with the intrinsic value of the company. If the stock is underpriced, a few of the negative consequences are that employees may be demoralized, the stock is less useful in stock acquisitions, and the firm may become a takeover target. If the stock is overpriced, the price will eventually fall, which will lead to a fall in employee morale and increased tension between the board of directors and the managers. Also, once the stock is overpriced, managers may engage in value-destroying activities in an attempt to prop up the stock price. Three ways many companies can improve investor communications are to (1) monitor the gap between price and intrinsic value, (2) understand the investor base, and (3) tailor communications to the investors who matter most.

In general, managers should try to communicate with sophisticated intrinsic investors because the activities of these investors have the most impact on the price of the stock. Managers should provide these investors with detailed financial reports as well as specific information on the individual businesses in the company. Managers should be honest and not use gimmicks such as changing the metrics reported each period to give the most favorable numbers. Furthermore, earnings guidance does not provide any discernible benefits.

1. In reporting financial information, companies should provide detailed income statement analysis for:
   A. Each unit down to at least EBITA.
   B. The whole aggregate firm to at least EBITA.
   C. Each unit's sales and cash costs.
   D. The whole aggregate firm's sales and cash costs.
2. With respect to transparency, which of the following statements are true?

I. Managers tend to avoid transparency for fear of revealing information that competitors can use.
II. Investors tend to reward firms that offer more transparency.
III. Managers respond to the increases in transparency of other firms.
IV. Managers respond to demands for increased transparency from investors.

A. I, II, and III only.
B. I, II, and IV only.
C. II, III, and IV only.
D. I, II, III, and IV.

3. With respect to growth versus value stocks, which of the following are true?

I. Most managers would like their firms to be growth stocks.
II. Growth stocks are those that have higher book and earnings multiples.
III. Most stocks labeled as growth stocks grow earnings and revenues faster than value stocks do.
IV. Most stocks labeled as growth stocks have higher ROICs.

A. I and II only.
B. II and III only.
C. I, II, and IV only.
D. I, III, and IV only.

4. Indicate in each of the following cases whether the statement concerning earnings guidance is True or False.

A. The total returns to shareholders (TRS) in the first year that managers begin to offer earnings guidance is no different from TRS at companies that don't offer guidance at all.
B. Managers engage in earnings guidance to lower share price volatility.
C. It has been proven that earnings guidance can increase liquidity.
D. For most industries, the firms that engage in earnings guidance have higher multiples such as enterprise-value/EBITA ratio.
E. Managers will gain advantages from providing guidance at the start of the financial year on the real short-, medium-, and long-term value drivers of their businesses.

5. Indicate in each of the following cases whether the statement concerning the type of information a firm should reveal is True or False.

A. A mining company should emphasize production targets more than expected commodity prices.

B. Multinational companies should discuss their targets using constant currency rates.

C. Managers of conglomerates should reveal aggregate numbers rather than business-by-business numbers.

D. Managers should provide ranges rather than point estimates.

E. Managers across industries should strive to provide information on a common set of value drivers.

6. Identify and describe two primary benefits that a systematic approach to investor communications provides a manager.

   A. ______________________________

   B. ______________________________

7. Identify the three objectives of sound investor communications.

   A. ______________________________

   B. ______________________________

   C. ______________________________

8. Identify and describe the three types of institutional investors.

   A. ______________________________

   B. ______________________________

   C. ______________________________

9. Why should investor relations executives understand the different types of institutional investors holding their company's stock?

10. Define the term *transparency* as it relates to corporate investor communications.

11. Why is it beneficial for a company to provide more information to the investors than is required by regulators and GAAP?

12. What do executives believe are the benefits of issuing EPS guidance? Are these benefits actually realized by companies?

13. Do markets reward companies with higher share prices when they consistently beat earnings consensus estimates? Explain.

31

Emerging Markets

Valuation is usually difficult in emerging markets because of unique risks and obstacles not present in developed markets. Additional considerations include macroeconomic uncertainty, illiquid capital markets, controls on the flow of capital into and out of the country, less rigorous standards of accounting and disclosure, and high levels of political risk. To estimate value in this environment, an analyst should use a triangulation approach based on values derived from three different methods: (1) a discounted cash flow (DCF) approach with probability-weighted scenarios that model the risks the business faces, (2) a DCF valuation with a country risk premium built into the cost of capital, and (3) a valuation based on comparable trading and transaction multiples.

The DCF approach is basically the same as that for a developed nation with additional steps. As in the case of developed nations, the analyst must develop consistent economic assumptions, forecast cash flows, and compute a WACC. Computing cash flows, however, may require extra work because of accounting differences. If done correctly, the two DCF methods should give the same estimate of value.

1. Match the items on the right to those on the left concerning an emerging market (there is an extra item on the right).

Country risk premium	___	A. U.S. Treasury bonds plus inflation difference
Risk-free rate	___	B. The multiples approach
A reason share price is below intrinsic value	___	C. Scenario DCF approach
Recommended primary method for determining value	___	D. A global market index
Recommended input for computing beta	___	E. Small free float
		F. The spread of the local government debt rate denominated in U.S. dollars and a U.S. government bond of similar maturity

2. In a two-scenario model of an emerging market, it is recommended that the analyst create a base-case set of forecasts and a set of forecasts associated with a period of economic distress. What range of probability weights is recommended to use for the economic distress scenario? Based on what evidence?

3. Although the cost of capital in emerging markets should be fairly close to a global cost of capital adjusted for local inflation and capital structure, there are five general guidelines to keep in mind. List those guidelines.

   A. ______________________________

   B. ______________________________

   C. ______________________________

   D. ______________________________

   E. ______________________________

4. Bill Smith and Jan Brown are analysts who are attempting to evaluate a company in an emerging market. Smith recommends creating one integrated set of economic and monetary assumptions and that they should spend extra effort to create the right forecasts. He lists the variables to be included in those assumptions. Brown cautions that the goal should not be to create the right forecasts and suggests a better approach.

   A. List the variables for which Smith would most likely wish to create assumptions.

   B. Instead of creating the right forecasts, what might Brown be recommending?

   C. To what extent should purchasing power parity (PPP) be an element in the forecasts of a company in an emerging market?

5. Given the following information, estimate the value of the company. The cash flows for the next year are estimated to be either $500 in the business-as-usual scenario or $200 in the distress scenario. The probabilities of the scenarios are 80 percent and 20 percent, respectively. The expected growth rate in cash flows in each case is 4 percent per year, and the cost of capital is 9 percent.

6. Estimate a country risk premium that is consistent with your answer in Question 5.

32

Valuing High-Growth Companies

The recommended, standard valuation principles apply to high-growth companies as well; however, there is a difference in the order of the steps of the valuation process and the emphasis on each step. The analyst should forecast the development of the company's markets and then work backward. As in the case of emerging markets, the analyst should create scenarios concerning the market's possible paths of development.

When looking into the future, the analyst should also estimate a point in time at which the company's performance is likely to stabilize and then work backward from that point. By then, the company will have captured a stable market share; and one part of the forecasting process requires determining the size of the market and the company's share. Then, the firm must estimate the inputs for return: operating margins, required capital investments, and ROIC. Finally, the analyst should develop scenarios and apply to the scenarios a set of probability weights consistent with long-term historical evidence on corporate growth.

1. The future state should be defined and bounded by measures of operating performance. List three examples of those measures of operating performance.

   A. ______________________________

   B. ______________________________

   C. ______________________________

2. List three possible methods for dealing with the uncertainty of high-growth companies. Indicate which method the text recommends and the reason why.

   A. ______________________________

   B. ______________________________

C. ______________________________

3. How should scenario weights be composed and calibrated?
4. How could scenario analysis be employed to gain a better understanding of the value drivers embedded in a high-growth firm?
5. Identify the key issues an analyst should consider when valuing start-up companies. How might an analyst resolve these issues?
6. An analyst computes the intrinsic values and probabilities for each of the indicated scenarios in the following table. Determine the expected intrinsic value and the value per share for this all equity financed firm.

Scenario	**Intrinsic value ($ million)**	**Probability**	**Intrinsic value × probability**
Success in both domestic and international markets	$2,500	0.3	
Success in domestic market	1,500	0.5	
Failure in domestic market	700	0.2	
Expected intrinsic value			
Shares outstanding: 20 million	Expected share price		

7. Referring to the previous question, suppose it is determined that the probability in the first, favorable scenario was too high, and the probability in the least favorable scenario was too low. The revised probabilities are 20 and 30 percent, respectively. Compute the new expected intrinsic value and value per share. What is the percent change in share price, and what does this say about the importance of scenario weights?

Scenario	**Intrinsic value ($ million)**	**Probability**	**Intrinsic value × probability**
Success in both domestic and international markets	$2,500	0.2	
Success in domestic market	1,500	0.5	
Failure in domestic market	700	0.3	
Expected intrinsic value			
Shares outstanding: 20 million	Expected share price		

33

Cyclical Companies

A cyclical company is one whose earnings demonstrate a repeating pattern of increases and decreases. The earnings of such companies fluctuate because of large changes in the prices of their products or changes in volume. Volatile earnings introduce additional complexity into the valuation process, as historical performance must be assessed in the context of the cycle.

Although the share prices of companies with cyclical earnings tend to be more volatile than those of less cyclical companies, their discounted cash flow (DCF) valuations are much more stable. Earnings forecasts may be the reason that the former is more volatile than the latter. Analysts' projections of the profits of cyclical companies are not very accurate, in that they tend not to forecast the downturns and generally have positive biases. Analysts may produce biased forecasts for these cyclical firms from fear of retaliation from the managers of the firms they analyze.

The behavior of managers may play a role in the cyclicality. They tend to increase and decrease investments at the same time (i.e., exhibit herd behavior). Three explanations for this behavior are (1) cash is generally more available when prices are high, (2) it is easier to get approval from boards of directors for investments when profits are high, and (3) executives get concerned about the possibilities of rivals growing faster than their firms.

The following steps outline one approach for evaluating a cyclical firm: (1) construct and value the normal cycle scenario using information about past cycles; (2) construct and value a new trend line scenario based on the recent performance of the company; (3) develop the economic rationale for each of the two scenarios, considering factors such as demand growth, companies entering or exiting the industry, and technology changes that will affect the balance of supply and demand; and (4) assign probabilities to the scenarios and calculate their weighted values.

1. List the three potential reasons that managers tend to increase and decrease investments at the same time (i.e., exhibit herd behavior).
   A. ______________________________
   B. ______________________________
   C. ______________________________
2. Simulations of capital expenditure timing have shown that the internal rates of return (IRRs) will be different for each of the following patterns. Rank them by placing 1, 2, 3, and 4 in the blanks to indicate which patterns exhibit the highest to lowest IRR.
   A. Spending evenly over cycle: __
   B. Optimally timed asset purchases: __
   C. Optimally timed capital spending: __
   D. Typical spending pattern: __
3. List the four steps for the recommended approach for evaluating a cyclical firm.
   A. ______________________________
   B. ______________________________
   C. ______________________________
   D. ______________________________
4. The point of the results in Exhibit 33.5 in the text is to illustrate how prices indicate that analysts:
   A. Make naive, random-walk forecasts, which are not very accurate.
   B. Make forecasts based on an extrapolation of recent trends.
   C. Make forecasts based on a 50/50 chance the firm will exhibit past cyclicality or break into a new trend.
   D. Should make naive, random-walk forecasts because they would beat most experts.
5. A pessimistic forecast from an analyst may damage the relationships of the analyst with which of the following?
   A. The analyst's employer.
   B. Investment banks.
   C. The managers of the analyzed firm.
   D. All of these.

For Questions 6 through 10, answer True or False.

6. The share prices of companies with cyclical earnings tend to be more volatile than those of less cyclical companies.

7. The discounted cash flow (DCF) valuations of companies with cyclical earnings are much less stable than those of less cyclical companies.
8. Consensus earnings forecasts for cyclical companies appear to include the effects of cyclicality.
9. Consensus earnings forecasts have shown an upward-sloping trend, whether the companies were at the peak or trough of the cycle.
10. Exhibit 33.6 illustrates that in the commodity chemical industry producer supply and not fluctuations in demand from customers is the cause of cyclicality in profits.

34

Banks

There are four complications in the valuation of banks: the latitude managers have with respect to accounting decisions, lack of transparency, the level of leverage, and the fact that banks are multibusiness companies. Those businesses include borrowing and lending, underwriting and placement of securities, payment services, asset management, proprietary trading, and brokerage.

In valuing a bank, the discounted cash flow (DCF) on operations approach is not appropriate because interest rates revenue and costs are part of operating income. The equity DCF method is more appropriate, and the analyst should triangulate the results with a multiples-based valuation. The equity approach uses a modified version of the value driver formula in which return on equity (ROE) and return on new equity (RONE) replace ROIC and RONIC, and net income replaces NOPLAT:

$$CV_t = \frac{NI_{t+1}\left(1 - \frac{g}{RONE}\right)}{k_e - g}$$

Problems associated with applying the equity DCF valuation method include determining the source of value, the effect of leverage, and the cost of holding equity capital. Economic spread analysis can help determine the sources of value creation. Other complications in bank valuations are monitoring the yield curve and forward rates, estimating loan loss provisions, approximating the bank's equity risk capital needs, and constructing separate statements for each of the bank's activities.

1. Which of the following best describes maturity mismatch and its role in bank operations?
   A. It refers to banks selling old loans so they can take on new loans, which earns a capital gain.

B. It refers to banks lending long-term and borrowing short-term, which earns positive net interest income.

C. It refers to the outdated accounting rules that most banks must operate under.

D. It refers to the inequality between accounting allowances for bad loans and the actual rate of losses on those loans.

2. Which of the following will change the cost of equity?

   I. Asset composition.

   II. Liability composition.

   III. The expected market return.

   IV. The risk-free rate.

   A. I and II only.

   B. I, III, and IV only.

   C. III and IV only.

   D. I, II, III, and IV.

3. The best method for understanding how much value a bank is creating in its different product lines is:

   A. Free cash flow analysis.

   B. Ratio analysis.

   C. Economic spread analysis.

   D. Net income analysis.

4. Up until the financial crises of 2008, which of the following was the usual ordering of the absolute value of the types of loan losses to banks?

   A. Credit card losses > mortgage losses > business loan losses.

   B. Mortgage losses > business loan losses > credit card losses.

   C. Credit card losses > business loan losses > mortgage losses.

   D. Mortgage losses > credit card losses > business loan losses.

5. Since the financial crises of 2010, which of the following has been the ordering of the absolute value of the types of loan losses to banks?

   A. Credit card losses > mortgage losses > business loan losses.

   B. Mortgage losses > business loan losses > credit card losses.

   C. Credit card losses > business loan losses > mortgage losses.

   D. Mortgage losses > credit card losses > business loan losses.

6. In the following list, identify whether the term relates to trading income or other income. Write "Trading" or "Other," respectively.

A. Real estate: ______________

B. Foreign exchange: ______________

C. Minority investments: ______________

D. Pension products: ______________

E. Bonds: ______________

F. Credit default swaps: ______________

G. Asset-backed obligations: ______________

7. Based on Exhibit 34.1 in the text, rank the sources of income for European banks from largest (1) to smallest (4). Indicate rankings for both 1988 and 2013. How have the relative sizes (as opposed to the rankings) changed?

	1988	2013
Commission income		
Interest income		
Trading income		
Other		

8. The following information is a simplified balance sheet of a bank. The relevant yields are 10 percent on loans, 2 percent on deposits, and a 4 percent intercompany interest rate on reserves for the spread model. Apply the latter rate to reserves and equity. The tax rate is 40 percent, and other expenses are $30.

Assets		**Liabilities**	
Cash reserves	$130	Deposits	$760
Loans	670	Equity	40
Total assets	800		

A. Calculate the net income with the income model:

Interest income	
Interest expense	
Other expenses	
Net profit before taxes	
Taxes	
Net income	

B. Calculate net income with the spread model:

Loan spread	
Deposit spread	
Equity spread	
Reserve debt	
Expenses	
Net profit before taxes	
Taxes	
Net income	

C. Compare the two models and demonstrate why they produce the same net income in this case.

9. The following is a set of forecasts of a bank for net income, changes in equity, and other comprehensive income or loss. The period 2016–2020 is the explicit forecast period. In the early years, the bank forecasts that it will have to raise new equity to lift its Tier 1 ratio from 6 to 9 percent, which will produce large decreases in equity. This will stabilize in 2019 and remain at a negative 11 in the foreseeable future. The other comprehensive income will remain at 2 in perpetuity beyond year 2019. Net income will be 90 in 2021 and is expected to grow at 2 percent thereafter. The return on new equity will be 10 percent. The required return on equity is 8 percent. Compute the present value of the forecasted cash flows.

Cash flow statement forecasts	**2016**	**2017**	**2018**	**2019**	**2020**
Net income	73	77	81	85	88
Increase or decrease in equity	−90	−90	−10	−11	−11
Other comprehensive income or loss	−1	0	1	2	2
Cash flow to equity					
				CV_{2020} =	
Cash flow value					
PV(CFE) =					

35

Flexibility

Net present values (NPVs) calculated from single cash flow projections may be inadequate because they do not take into account the ability to expand or scale back. The following is a simple example where a firm can scale back by eliminating a negative cash flow project after the first period. There is a 60 percent probability of \$20 per year forever or 40 percent probability of –\$6 per year forever. The discount rate is 10 percent. If the initial cost today is \$100, then without an option to cancel the NPV would be:

$$-\$100 + 0.6 \times (\$20/0.10) + 0.4 \times (-\$6/0.10) = -\$4$$

With the option to abandon after the first year, the NPV would be:

$$-\$100 + 0.6 \times (\$20/0.10) + 0.4 \times (-\$6/1.10) = \$17.82$$

The value of the option to cancel the project is the difference, or \$21.82.

The inclusion of flexibility into the analysis is generally more relevant in the valuation of individual businesses and projects. The real-option valuation (ROV) and decision tree analysis (DTA) are the two primary methods of valuation. Both depend on forecasting based on contingent states of the world. Although ROV is often a better methodology to use than DTA, it is not the right approach in every case.

1. The value of flexibility is greatest when:
   A. Uncertainty is high and managers can react to new information.
   B. Uncertainty is low and managers can react to new information.
   C. Uncertainty is high and managers cannot react to new information.
   D. Uncertainty is low and managers cannot react to new information.

2. The option to defer an investment is most like:
   A. A futures contract on a bond.
   B. A swap contract.
   C. A put option on a stock.
   D. A call option on a stock.
3. The option to abandon an investment is most like:
   A. A futures contract on a bond.
   B. A swap contract.
   C. A put option on a stock.
   D. A call option on a stock.
4. A project has a 50/50 chance of generating either a positive cash flow of $1 per year forever or a zero cash flow. The discount rate is 5 percent. If the initial cost is $10, what is the NPV with the option to stop after the first year?
   A. –$10
   B. $0
   C. $10
   D. $20
5. In the event tree used in the binomial approach to option valuation, at each node the value either increases or decreases by the proportion u or d, respectively. If the standard deviation is 10 percent per year and the horizon is six months, what are the up-movement u and down-movement d values?
   A. 1.0488 and 0.9534
   B. 1.0513 and 0.9511
   C. 1.0733 and 0.9317
   D. 1.2505 and 0.8000
6. Explain why a change in interest rates can produce either an increase or a decrease in the value of a project with the flexibility to expand.
   A. Increase in value because: ____________________
   B. Decrease in value because: ____________________
7. To recognize opportunities for creating value from flexibility when assessing investment projects or strategies, managers should ask the following three questions concerning three important details.
   A. ____________________
   B. ____________________
   C. ____________________

8. Outline the four-step process for valuing flexibility.

   A. ____
   ____

   B. ____
   ____

   C. ____
   ____

   D. ____
   ____

9. A project costs $500 to start and has a 10 percent chance of generating $400 per year forever and a 90 percent chance of generating $50 per year forever. The discount rate is 25 percent. In one year, the investor has the right to expand and start eight more similar projects. What is the NPV with and without the option to expand?

10. A product will have a NPV equal to $4,000 if successful in two years. There is a 20 percent chance it will pass the research phase, which will be determined after the first year, and a 50 percent chance it will pass the testing phase at the end of the second year. The initial costs for getting the research phase started are $240. If it passes the research phase, there will be a required investment of $100. If it passes the testing phase, there will be a required investment of $200. The discount rate for the project is 20 percent, and the risk-free rate is 4 percent. Compute the standard NPV and the NPV including the flexibility.

Part Two

Solutions

1

Why Value Value?

1. Data from both Europe and the United States found that companies that created the most shareholder value showed *stronger* employment growth.
2. In the past 30 years, there have been at least *six* financial crises that arose largely because companies and banks were *financing illiquid assets with short-term debt.*
3. Two activities that managers often use in an attempt to increase share price but that do not actually create value are changes in *capital structure (or financing of the firm)* and changes in *accounting practices.*
4. Maximizing current share price is not equivalent to maximizing long-term value because *managers, who know more than shareholders about the firm's prospects, could slash crucial expenses to improve the stock price in the short term. Eventually, this will catch up to the firm, and the long term stock price will suffer.*
5. During the Internet boom of the late 1990s, many firms lost sight of value creation principles by blindly pursuing *getting bigger* without *maintaining a competitive advantage.*
6. B
7. D
8. B
9. C
10. D

2

Fundamental Principles of Value Creation

1.

Types of growth	Ranking
A. Increase share in a growing market.	1. D
B. Expand an existing market.	2. B
C. Acquire businesses.	3. A
D. Introduce new products to market.	4. C

2. High-ROIC companies typically create more value by *focusing on growth*, while lower-ROIC companies create more value by *increasing ROIC*.
3. Most often in mature companies, a low ROIC indicates *a flawed business model or unattractive industry structure.*
4. Earnings and cash flow are often *correlated*, but earnings don't tell the whole story of value creation, and focusing too much on earnings or earnings growth *can lead to straying away from the value-creating path.*
5. When ROIC is greater than the cost of capital, the relationship between growth and value is *positive*. When ROIC is less than the cost of capital, the relationship between growth and value is *negative*. When ROIC equals the cost of capital, the relationship between growth and value is *zero*.
6. With respect to countries, the core valuation principle is *applicable*, as made evident by the fact that U.S. companies trade *at higher multiples than* companies in other countries.
7. When comparing the effect of an increase in growth on a high-ROIC company and a low-ROIC company, a 1 percent increase in growth will have *a higher positive effect on the high-ROIC company.*

8. At high levels of ROIC, improving ROIC by increasing margins will create *much more* value than an equivalent ROIC increase by improving capital productivity.
9. Economic profit is the spread between *the return on invested capital* and *the cost of capital* times *the amount of invested capital.*
10. D. Investment rate = Growth/ROIC = 2%/10% = 20%.
11. C.

$$\text{Value} = \frac{\$300\left(1 - \frac{.05}{.15}\right)}{.13 - .05} = \$2,500$$

3

Conservation of Value and the Role of Risk

1. Changing capital structure creates value only if it *improves cash flows or lowers the cost of capital.*
2. An acquisition will create value only if it increases cash flows by *reducing costs, increasing revenue growth, or improving the use of fixed or working capital.*
3. For publicly traded companies, nondiversifiable risk affects the *cost of capital,* and diversifiable risk *does not.*
4. Diversifiable risk arises from *firm-specific factors, such as fluctuations in demand for a firm's products, the ability to retain talented management, and rising input costs.*
5. Managers should hedge only risks that are *not part of the core business.*
6. Managers should not take on cash flow risk that *has a measurable probability of bankrupting the company.*
7. When the likelihood of investing cash at *low returns* is *high,* share repurchases make sense as a tactic for avoiding value destruction.
8. Financial engineering is the use of financial instruments or structures, other than straight debt and equity, to manage a company's capital structure and risk profile.
9. Because interest expense is tax deductible, share repurchases can have the beneficial effect of *increasing earnings per share,* but this may not increase share price because *the price-to-earnings (P/E) ratio may decline.*
10. Studies of share repurchases have shown that companies *aren't very good* at timing share repurchases, often buying when *their share prices are high, not low.*

4

The Alchemy of Stock Market Performance

Percentage	Traditional	Enhanced
Growth	10.0	10.0
Required investment		(3.3)
TRS from performance		6.7
Zero-growth return		8.3
Change in P/E	5.0	5.0
Dividend yield	5.0	
TRS	20.0	20.0

1. D. TRS from performance = $(E_1/E_0 - 1) - (K_1/K_0 - 1)$ = ($22/$20 – 1) – ($206.6/$200 – 1) = 6.7%.
2. C. Dividend yield = (D_1/EV_0) = $12/$240 = 5%.
3. A. Zero-growth return = 1/12 = 8.3%.
4. D. TRS = 10% + 5.0% + 5.0% = 20.0%.
5. The components in the two-component breakdown are:
   A. Percent change in share price.
   B. Percent change in dividend yield.

   The components in the three-component breakdown are:

   A. Percent change in earnings.
   B. Percent change in P/E.
   C. Percent change in dividend yield.

6. For periods of *10–15* years or more, it is true that if managers focus on *improving TRS to win performance bonuses,* then their interests and the interests of shareholders should be aligned.
7. The detrimental result of the expectations treadmill is that, for firms that have had superior operating and TRS performance, the managers who try to continually meet the higher expectations may engage in detrimental activities such as *ill-advised acquisitions* or *new ventures.*
8. A company should measure management performance in terms of the company's performance, not its share price. Three areas of focus should be *growth, ROIC,* and *TRS performance relative to peers.*

5

The Stock Market Is Smarter Than You Think

1. C
2. D
3. C
4. A
5. D
6. B – This particularly applies to companies from emerging countries.
7. A
8. C
9. C
10. C
11. True
12. False
13. True
14. A
15. C
16. D
17. A
18. B

6

Return on Invested Capital

1. Porter's five forces are:
   A. Threat of entry.
   B. Pressure from substitute products.
   C. Bargaining power of buyers.
   D. Bargaining power of suppliers.
   E. The degree of rivalry among existing competitors.
2. The key driver of ROIC is *competitive advantage*.
3. Companies have been fairly successful in sustaining their rates of ROIC.
4. In the context of competitive advantage and ROIC, quality means a real or perceived difference between one product or service and another that prompts consumers to pay a higher price.
5. For a pricing advantage, using rational pricing discipline requires either a *price leader that all other producers follow* or *barriers to entry*.
6. The two terms (economies of scale and scalable products) are similar, but they are not the same. If a firm has economies of scale, then its average costs decline as output increases. If a firm has scalable products, then its additional costs for producing the product are essentially zero for each additional unit of output. An example is the delivery of physical goods and the delivery of information via the Internet. Physical goods require a cost for delivery, but that cost to a given location would be lower for each additional unit in a given delivery. In the delivery of information, the first and last unit would have about the same delivery cost, which would be essentially zero.
7. Between 1963 and the early 2000s, the median ROIC was about *10* percent, and the interquartile range was from *5* percent to *20* percent.

8. Since the early 2000s, the median ROIC was about *16* percent, and the interquartile range was from *6* percent to *35* percent.
9. The increase in median ROIC and the widening of the distribution of ROICs are the result of *a change in the composition of U.S. firms. A higher percentage of firm profits is coming from high-ROIC sectors, such as information technology, medical devices, and pharmaceuticals.*
10. The reason for the increasing difference between ROIC without goodwill and ROIC including goodwill is *that acquiring firms are paying higher premiums that reflect the value they expect to add to the acquired firm.*
11. Rank of industry based on ROIC:

A. Paper, forest products	1. B
B. Pharmaceuticals	2. D
C. Consumer staples	3. C
D. Health care equipment, supplies	4. A

The median ROICs for A, B, C and D are about 6 percent, 40 percent, 20 percent, and 28 percent, respectively.

12. B. ROICs tend to be mean reverting, but firms tend to sustain their relative position to the mean (i.e., either higher or lower) for 10 years or more.
13. A. 6.8 percent.

$$\text{ROIC} = (1 - 0.32)\frac{\$3.40 - \$1.80}{\$16} = 0.068$$

14. C. For cereal manufacturers and meat producers, the ROICs are 30 percent and 15 percent, respectively. Cereal manufacturers earn a higher return as a result of being able to brand their products.

7

Growth

1. The two sources of organic growth are (1) portfolio momentum or increase in the size of the market and (2) increasing market share. Market growth is the largest driver of growth, followed by mergers and acquisitions and market share growth.
2. Incremental innovation will rarely create lasting value, because competitors can easily retaliate. Competitors can either lower the prices on their existing products or, if the innovator raises the price of the improved product, keep their prices the same. Also, the rivals can also come up with their own incremental innovations, which is easier than coming up with a new product or service.
3. With respect to product development, growth is difficult to maintain because for each product *that is maturing and reaching its peak in revenue*, the company must *develop a new product that will grow faster to replace it*. This is called the *portfolio treadmill* effect.
4. Publicly traded firms have grown at a higher rate than GDP. The two reasons for this are:
   A. Publicly traded firms can grow faster because of their ease in raising capital, so their growth can be higher than the overall economy at the expense of nonpublic firms.
   B. Public firms have experienced higher growth from expanding sales to overseas markets, and expanding markets and bringing in new consumers are the most effective means of growing and creating value.
5. B
6. D
7. A
8. B

9. A
10. C
11. D
12. A

8

Frameworks for Valuation

1. Value of the equity = PV(FCFs) + Nonoperating assets – Nonequity claims.

   Value of the equity = \$400m + \$9m – \$220m – \$33m = \$156m.

   Value of each share of common stock = \$156m/2m = \$78.

2. Value of the equity = Discounted economic profit + Invested capital + Nonoperating assets – Nonequity claims.

   Value of the equity = \$150m + \$250m + \$16m – \$80m – \$26m.

   Value of each share of common stock = \$310m.

3. C
4. A
5. Economic profit = Invested capital × (ROIC – WACC).

   Economic profit = \$300m × (12% – 10.5%) = \$4.5m.

6. The Modigliani-Miller proposition says that without the effect of taxes, the capital structure should not affect the value of the firm. The adjusted present value model computes the value of the firm as if it were all-equity financed and then adds the value of the debt tax shield.

7.

Source of capital	Proportion of total capital	Cost of capital	Marginal tax rate	After-tax cost of capital	Contribution to WACC
Debt	42%	6.2%	34%	*4.09%*	*1.72%*
Equity	58%	9.8%		*9.8%*	*5.68%*
WACC					*7.40%*

8. Since the cash flows and the tax shields will grow at a constant rate, the value of each can be estimated with the constant growth model. Both are discounted using the unlevered cost of equity.

$$V = \$40m/(9\% - 5\%) + \$9m/(9\% - 3\%) = \$1,150m$$

9.

Year	Free cash flow (FCF)	Interest tax shield (ITS)	Discount factor	PV of FCF	PV of ITS
2016	402	31	0.9174	368.8	28.4
2017	420	32	0.8417	353.5	26.9
2018	436	34	0.7722	336.7	26.3
Continuing value	8,900	380	0.7722	6,872.4	293.4
Present value	7,931.4	375.0			
PV of free cash flow	7,931.4				
PV of interest tax shield	375.0				
PV of free cash flow and interest tax shield	8,306.4				
Midyear adjustment factor	365.7				
Value of operations	8,672.1				
Value of long-term investments	155				
Value of tax loss carryforwards	81				
Enterprise value	8,908.1				
Value of debt	2,583				
Value of capitalized operating leases	1,674				
Equity value	4,651.1				

9

Reorganizing the Financial Statements

1. A
2. D
3. B
4. B
5. C. $17,857 = $5,000/(0.08 + 1/5).
6. A $200 = Working cash + receivables = (2% × $5,000) + $100
7. B
8. Total funds invested = OA – OL + NOA = $400 – $60 + $100 + $50 = $490 = D + $30 + $200. Debt = $260.
9. Given the accounting income statement on the left, enter the appropriate entries into the NOPLAT worksheet on the right and compute income available to investors. The marginal tax rate is 30 percent.

Revenues	$2,000	Revenues	$2,000
Operating costs	(1,000)	Operating costs	(1,000)
Depreciation	(400)	Depreciation	(400)
Operating profit	$600	Operating profit	$600
Interest	(40)	Operating taxes	(180)
Nonoperating income	10	NOPLAT	420
Earnings before taxes	$570	After-tax nonoperating income	7
Taxes	(171)	Income available to investors	$427
Net income	$399		

Adding back the after-tax interest expense of \$28 = (1 – 0.3) \$40 to net income gives the income available to investors, which shows that the adjustments are correct.

10. NOPLAT = \$35.0
Working capital = \$44
Invested capital = \$194
Total funds invested = \$199

NOPLAT	**Year**	**Total funds invested**	**Year**
Revenues	200.0	Working cash	10
Cost of sales	(80.0)	Accounts receivable	30
Selling costs	(50.0)	Inventories	10
Depreciation	(20.0)	Accounts payable	(6)
Operating profit	50.0	**Working capital**	**44**
Operating taxes	(15.0)	Property, plant, and equipment	150
NOPLAT	**35.0**	**Invested capital**	**194**
		Prepaid pension assets	5
Reconciliation of NOPLAT		Total funds invested	199
Net income	32.2		
After-tax interest expense	(2.8)	*Reconciliation of total funds invested*	
After-tax gain on sale	–	Short-term debt	12
NOPLAT	35.0	Long-term debt	70
		Restructuring reserves	7
		Debt and debt equivalents	89
		Equity	110
		Total funds invested	**199**

10

Analyzing Performance

1. ROE mixes operating performance with capital structure.
   ROA includes nonoperating assets, and it ignores the benefits of accounts payable and other operating liabilities.
2. D
3. C. ROIC = (1 – 0.25) × (3,000/24,000) × (24,000/20,000) = 11.25%.
4. A. Operating profit margin = (3,000/24,000) = 12.5%; capital turnover = (24,000/20,000) = 1.2.
5. A
6. C
7. B
8. C
9.

	EBIT	EBITDA	EBITDAR
2015	interest	interest	(interest + rental expense)
Numerator	48	187	187
Denominator	39	39	39
Ratio	1.23	4.79	4.79
	EBIT	**EBITDA**	**EBITDAR**
2016	interest	interest	(interest + rental expense)
Numerator	20	156	404
Denominator	30	30	278
Ratio	0.667	5.20	1.45

10. Days = 365 × (Cash/revenues).
    Cash = Current assets – (Receivables + Inventories + Other current assets).
    Cash = $863 – $523 = $340.
    Days = 365 × ($340/$4,056) = 30.60 days.

11

Forecasting Performance

1. True
2. True
3. False
4. False
5. True
6. B
7. C
8. C
9. C
10. A
11. The problem is that the parent company can record only the dividends received and not the entire cash and revenue received from the investments. The analyst cannot use traditional drivers for these investments, but instead must estimate future nonoperating income by examining historical growth in nonoperating income or by examining the revenue and profit forecasts of publicly traded companies that are comparable to the equity investment.
12. Top-down forecast:

    A. Step 1: Size the whole market.

    B. Step 2: Determine market share.

    C. Step 3: Forecast prices.

    Bottom-up forecast:

    A. Input 1: Estimate demand from existing customers.

    B. Input 2: Estimate customer turnover.

    C. Input 3: Estimate potential for new customers.

13.

Typical Forecast Drivers for the Income Statement	Line item	Typical forecast driver	Typical forecast ratio
Operating	Cost of goods sold	Revenue	COGS/revenue
	Selling, general, and administrative expense	Revenue	SG&A/revenue
	Depreciation	Prior-year net PP&E	Depreciationt/ net $PP\&E_{t-1}$
Nonoperating	Interest expense	Prior-year to total debt	Interest expenset/total $debt_{t-1}$
	Interest income	Prior-year to excess cash	Interest incomet/excess $cash_{t-1}$

14.

	2015	2016		2015	2016
Revenue growth		20%	Revenues	500	600
Cost of goods sold/ revenue	40%	40%	Cost of goods sold	(200)	(240)
Selling and general expenses/revenues	30%	20%	Selling and general expenses	(150)	(120)
Depreciation/net PP&E	20%	30%	Depreciation	(56)	(100.8)
EBITA/revenues			EBITA	94	139.2
Interest rate					
Interest expense/total debt	10%	8%	Interest expense	(40)	(35.2)
Interest income/excess cash	6%	5%	Interest income	12	10
			Nonoperating income	10	13
Nonoperating items			Earnings before taxes	76	127
Nonoperating income growth		30%			

	2015	2016		2015	2016
			Provision for income taxes	(22.8)	(38.1)
Taxes			Net income	53.2	88.9
Average tax rate	30%	30%			
	2014	**2015**		**2014**	**2015**
Assets			Liabilities and equity		
Operating cash	10	10	Accounts payable	20	24
Excess cash	200	200	Short-term debt	300	330
Inventory	60	72	Current liabilities	320	354
Current assets	270	282			
			Long-term debt	100	110
Net PP&E	280	336	Common stock	80	80
Equity investments	100	100	Retained earnings	150	174
Total assets	650	718	Total liabilities and equity	650	718

12

Estimating Continuing Value

1. True
2. False
3. False
4. True
5. False
6. C
7. A
8. A
9. B
10. A
11. A. Multiples: The company will be worth some multiple of book value or price-to-earnings.

    B. Liquidation value: The company will be worth the value of proceeds from the sale of assets at the end of the explicit forecast period after paying the liabilities.

    C. Replacement cost: The continuing value equals what it would take to purchase the firm's assets at the end of the forecast period.
12.

$$CV_t = \frac{NOPLAT_{t+1}\left[1 - \frac{g}{RONIC}\right]}{WACC - g}$$

$$CV_t = \frac{\$200\left[1 - \frac{0.04}{0.10}\right]}{0.08 - 0.04} = \$3,000$$

13.

$$CV_t = \frac{IC_t\,(ROIC_t - WACC)}{WACC} + \frac{PV\left(\text{Economic Profit}_{t+2}\right)}{WACC - g}$$

$$PV\left(\text{Econimic Profit}_{t+2}\right) = \frac{NOPLAT_{t+1}\left[\frac{g}{RONIC}\right](RONIC - WACC)}{WACC}$$

$$PV\left(\text{Econimic Profit}_{t+2}\right) = \frac{\$240\left[\frac{0.02}{0.10}\right](0.10 - 0.07)}{0.07} = \$20.57$$

$$CV_t = \frac{\$2,000\,(0.12 - 0.07)}{0.07} + \frac{\$20.57}{0.07 - 0.02}$$

$$CV_t = \$1,428.57 + \$411.43 = \$1,840.00$$

14.

	Year 1	**Year 2**	**Year 3**	**CV**	**Key value drivers**	
Revenues	$200.0	$210.0	$216.0	$220.0	Investment rate	60.0%
Operating costs	(180.0)	(189.0)	(194.4)	(198.0)	Return on new capital	15.0%
Operating margin	$20.0	$21.0	$21.6	$22.0	Growth rate	9.0%
Operating taxes	(6.0)	(6.3)	(6.5)	(6.6)	Operating costs as percent of sales	90.0%
NOPLAT	$14.0	$14.7	$15.1	$15.4	Operating taxes	30.0%
					NOPLAT margin	7.0%
Net investment	(8.4)	(8.8)	(9.1)			
Free cash flow	$5.6	$5.9	$6.0	$205.3	ROIC	14.0%
					Cost of capital	12.0%
Discounted cash flow						
Discount factor	0.893	0.797	0.712	0.712		
Discounted cash flow	$5.0	$4.7	$4.3	$146.2		
Value of operations	$160.2					

13

Estimating the Cost of Capital

1. D
2. B
3. C
4. B
5. A
6. C
7. D
8. In the aftermath of the financial crisis of 2008, the U.S. Federal Reserve and several other central banks throughout the world lowered interest rates to historically low levels and simultaneously bought trillions of dollars of government bonds. Together, these actions pushed yields on government bonds to near zero. This poses a challenge in estimating the firm's cost of equity, as these yields are typically used as an estimate of the (nominal) risk-free rate. One can create a synthetic risk-free rate to address this by adding the expected inflation rate to the long-term historical average real risk-free rate.
9. Unlevered beta for Firm A = $0.7/1.4 = 0.50$

   Unlevered beta for Firm B = $1.2/3.0 = 0.40$

   Industry beta = $0.45 = (0.50 + 0.40)/2$

   Equity beta for Firm A = $0.45 \times 1.4 = 0.63$

   Equity beta for Firm B = $0.45 \times 3 = 1.35$

10. $D/E = 1.0 \rightarrow D/(D+E) = E/(D+E) = 0.50$

    $WACC = [0.5 \times 6\% \times (1 - 0.4)] + [0.5 \times 10\%] = 6.8\%$

11. $V = (1{,}500{,}000 \times \$10) + (8{,}000 \times \$1{,}125) = \$24{,}000{,}000$

    The weights are

    $E/V = 15{,}000{,}000/24{,}000{,}000 = 0.625$

    $D/V = 9{,}000{,}000/24{,}000{,}000 = 0.375$

    $WACC = [0.375 \times 9\% \times (1 - 0.34)] + [0.625 \times 12\%] = 9.73\%$

14

Moving from Enterprise Value to Value per Share

1. B
2. A
3. C
4. B
5. D
6. D
7. In order of listing,

$$\text{Value of the firm} = \$320\text{m} + \$25\text{m} - \$2\text{m} - \$185\text{m} + \$2\text{m} - \$4\text{m} - \$6\text{m} = \$150\text{m}$$

$$\text{Value per share} = \$150\text{m}/(2\text{m shares}) = \$75/\text{share}$$

8.

Excess real estate	+
Preferred stock	–
Noncontrolling interest	–
Tax loss carry-forward	+
Unfunded pension liabilities	–
Nonconsolidated subsidiaries	+

9. Is book value a reasonable approximation for evaluating the asset or liability?
   A. Yes
   B. No

C. Yes

D. No

E. No

F. Yes

G. No

H. No

10. A. The subsidiary is not publicly traded, and the stake is less than 20 percent of the value of the subsidiary.

    B. The tracking portfolio method.

15

Analyzing the Results

1. C
2. B
3. A. Unadjusted financial statements: The balance sheet should balance each year, and the dividends and retained earnings should be congruous with net income.

   B. Rearranged financial statements: The sum of invested capital plus nonoperating assets equals the cumulative sources of financing. NOPLAT is the same when calculated from the top down or from the bottom up.

   C. Statement of cash flows: The excess cash and debt line up with the cash flow statement.
4. A. The sensitivity of the results to broad economic conditions.

   B. The level of competitiveness of the industry.

   C. The internal capabilities of the company to achieve the forecasts of output and growth.

   D. The ability of the company to raise the necessary capital from the markets.
5. Three examples of trade-offs are:

   A. Sales and prices.

   B. Lower inventory and higher sales.

   C. Higher growth and lower margin.
6. When using the scenario approach, an analyst should not shortcut the process by deducting the face value of debt from the scenario-weighted

value of operations because *this would seriously underestimate the equity value, as the value of debt is different in each scenario.*

7. A.

	Year 1	Year 2	Year 3
Number of units	200	220	242
Price per unit	$100	$104	$110
Cost per unit	$90	$90	$90
Income	$2,000	$3,080	$4,840
Invested capital	$20,000	$21,000	$22,540
ROIC	10.00%	14.67%	21.47%

B. These results are not realistic for a competitive industry because the ROIC becomes too high. It is likely that competitors would enter the market and lower sales and/or depress prices.

8. A.

	Year 1	Year 2	Year 3
Number of units	200	220	242
Price per unit	$100	$104	$110
Cost per unit	$90	$93.6	$99
Net income	$2,000	$2,288	$2,662
Invested capital	$20,000	$21,000	$22,144
ROIC	10.00%	10.90%	12.02%

B.

	Year 1	Year 2	Year 3
Number of units	200	200	200
Price per unit	$100	$104	$110
Cost per unit	$90	$90	$90
Net income	$2,000	$2,800	$4,000
Invested capital	$20,000	$21,000	$22,400
ROIC	10.00%	13.33%	17.86%

9. Based on these results, the constant costs assumption seems to be responsible for the high ROIC. When costs increase with inflation, the ROIC increases to only 12.02 percent.

16

Using Multiples

1. C
2. A
3. C
4. D
5. PEG ratio = 15/5 = 3.0. Although popular with some analysts, this multiple doesn't take into consideration ROIC, which has a significant impact on a company's valuation. Additionally, there is no mathematical derivation showing that this is a meaningful metric. Finally, there is no standardized approach for the time horizon for growth for PEG ratios.
6. $$\frac{\text{Value}}{\text{EBITA}} = \frac{(1-T)\left(1-\frac{g}{\text{ROIC}}\right)}{\text{WACC}-g} = \frac{(1-0.34)\left(1-\frac{.04}{.10}\right)}{0.09-0.04} = 7.92$$
7. The measure should remove nonconsolidated subsidiaries and excess cash from the enterprise value:

$$\frac{\text{Value}}{\text{EBITA}} = \frac{(\$600 + \$300 - \$100 - \$50)}{\$100} = 7.5$$

8. A. Production methodology: capital intensive versus capital light.
   B. Distribution channels: online versus bricks and mortar.
   C. Research and development: internal versus acquired.
9. A. EBITA is superior to EBIT because amortization is a measure determined by past acquisitions. It does not affect future cash flows, and therefore it should not be included in the operating earnings measure.

B. EBITA is superior to EBITDA because the earnings measure should include depreciation. Although analysts often exclude depreciation because it is a noncash measure reflecting past cash outflows, depreciation is important in this case because it gives an indication of what will have to be invested in the future to replace the existing assets.

10. Examples of nonfinancial ratios include ratios of value to web site hits, value to unique visitors, and value to number of subscribers. These measures had some explanatory power for prices in the early years of the wave of Internet companies. After the industry matured, they lost power relative to the explanatory power of gross profit and R&D spending.
11. Although enterprise to EBITA is commonly used, when tax rates are different, NOPLAT is a better measure to use. An extreme example is U.S. oil and gas pipeline companies. Those pipeline companies that are organized as master limited partnerships (MLPs) do not pay any corporate income taxes, while other firms pay up to a 35 percent tax rate. Since the tax differences represent real cash flows, they should not be ignored.

17

Valuing by Parts

1. C
2. A
3. C
4. The steps in valuing a multibusiness company by parts are:
   A. Understanding the mechanics of and insights from valuing a company by the sum of its parts
   B. Building financial statements by business unit—based on incomplete information, if necessary
   C. Estimating the weighted average cost of capital by business unit
   D. Testing the value based on multiples of peers
5. The issues an analyst encounters when creating financial statements for business units are:
   A. Allocating corporate overhead costs
   B. Dealing with intercompany transactions
   C. Understanding financial subsidiaries
   D. Navigating incomplete public information
6. Three best practices for testing valuation by parts based on multiples of peers are:
   A. Eliminating outliers
   B. Using medians of "close" peers
   C. Using NOPLAT instead of using EBITA
7. False
8. True
9. True
10. False

11. This is not an appropriate technique to use unless the ROIC and growth projections for the three divisions are all the same. This is quite unlikely. It's more likely that each division will have unique ROIC and growth dynamics that would lead to one division being worth more than another. For instance, if Division A had long-term projections for ROIC of 20 percent, WACC of 10 percent, and growth of 6 percent while Division B's respective projections were 10 percent, 11 percent, and 3 percent, Division A would have a significantly higher valuation, which can be verified using the below formula.

$$CV_t = \frac{NOPLAT_{t+1}\left[1 - \frac{g}{ROIC}\right]}{WACC - g}$$

12. This is not an appropriate technique to use unless the ROIC and growth projections for the three divisions are all the same. This is quite unlikely. Funds should be allocated based on the ROIC and growth projections. For instance, if one of the divisions has an ROIC significantly above its WACC, then this division should receive a greater balance of the funds (assuming that these funds can be put to use at the relatively high ROIC level).

18

Taxes

1. True
2. False
3. True
4. True
5. True
6. False
7. True
8. False
9.

Account	DTA or DTL?	Operating or nonoperating?
Nondeductible intangibles	DTL	Nonoperating
Tax loss carryforwards	DTA	Nonoperating
Accelerated depreciation	DTL	Operating
Pension and postretirement benefits	DTA	Nonoperating
Warranty reserves	DTA	Operating

10.

	Domestic subsidiary	Foreign subsidiary	R&D tax credits	One-time credits	Company
EBITA	3,000	800			3,800
Amortization	(1,000)	(200)			(1,200)
EBIT	2,000	600			2,600
Interest expense	(800)	(200)			(1,000)
Gains on asset sales	100	0			100
Earnings before taxes	1,300	400			1,700
Taxes	(390)	(160)	110	88	(352)
Net income	910	240			1,348
Tax rates (percent)					
Statutory rate	30%	40%			
Effective tax rate					20.7%
EBITA	3,000	800			3,800
Operating taxes	(900)	(320)	110		(1,110)
NOPLAT	2,100	480	110		2,690
Tax rates (percent)					
Statutory rate	30%	40%			
Operating tax rate					29.2%

19

Nonoperating Items, Provisions, and Reserves

1.
   A. No
   B. Yes
   C. No
   D. No
   E. Yes
   F. Yes
   G. No
   H. No
   I. No
2. **NOPLAT**

Reported EBITA	$4,000
Interest associated with plant decommissioning	500
Increase in income smoothing reserve	600
NOPLAT	$5,100

Invested Capital

Reserve for plant decommissioning	$ 5,000
Reserve for restructuring	1,000
Reserve for income smoothing	2,500
Equity	10,000
Invested capital	$18,500

ROIC = $5,100/$18,500 = 27.57%

3.

Balance sheet	Year 1	Year 2	Year 3
Starting reserve	0	30.80	64.07
Plant-decommissioning expense	30.80	30.80	30.80
Interest cost	0	2.47	5.13
Decommissioning payout	0	0	(100)
Ending reserve	30.80	64.07	0
Income statement			
Reported provision	30.80	33.27	35.93

4. FASB and IFRS rules require that acquisition premiums be separated into goodwill and intangible assets. In-process R&D is an intangible asset of indefinite life.
5. If a company routinely has to defend itself against litigation, then the charges should be operating charges. An example would likely be in the service industry, most notably a hospital, which may frequently have to defend itself against litigation.
6. It is recommended to treat goodwill impairments as nonoperating and then add back cumulative impairments to goodwill on the balance sheet. Since the purpose of computing ROIC with goodwill is to measure historical performance, including all past acquisition premiums, goodwill should remain at its original level.
7. Whether to make an adjustment to NOPLAT for such an expense depends on whether the charge is large enough to affect perceptions of performance. Making the effort to adjust NOPLAT is recommended only if the adjustment is significant. It is not recommended to make adjustments if they are small, because such adjustments could make the analysis overly complex and time-consuming.

8.

Examples of provisions and reserves	Classification treatment	Treatment in NOPLAT	Treatment in invested capital	Treatment in valuation
Plant decommissioning costs and unfunded retirement plans	D	E	J or K	P
Provisions for the sole purpose of income smoothing	B	G	L	O

Examples of provisions and reserves	**Classification treatment**	**Treatment in NOPLAT**	**Treatment in invested capital**	**Treatment in valuation**
Product returns and warranties	C	H	I	M
Restructuring charges (e.g., expected severance payouts from layoffs)	A	F	J or K	N

20

Leases and Retirement Obligations

1. A profitable company has chosen to lease its assets and account for them as operating leases. This move will artificially *lower* operating profits. It will artificially *increase* capital productivity. With respect to return, it is most likely that it will *increase* ROIC.
2. The analyst's adjustments should *increase* assets, *increase* liabilities, and *increase* operating income.
3. The interest rate for operating lease adjustments is usually lower than the firm's cost of debt. This is because that interest expense is secured with the leased assets.
4. An analyst would probably have to get the information on rental expenses from the company's footnotes because it is usually not explicitly shown as a separate line item on the income statement. The analyst would have to estimate the value of the asset because the value is usually not disclosed.
5. Asset value = \$4,000/(0.06 + 1/5) = \$4,000/0.26 = \$15,384.61.
6. The analyst can multiply the rental expense by a capitalization rate. Many analysts in the investment banking industry multiply rental expenses by 8 times to approximate asset value. Although based on reasonable assumptions, the method is very simple and can both overvalue and undervalue the leased assets.
7. A. The use of more operating leases led to agencies awarding lower credit ratings, and both combined to increase the required yields on new public bond issuances.

B. Interest rates on unrated, unsecured debt were explained better by credit statistics adjusted for operating leases.

C. All three groups (investors, lenders, and rating agencies) tend to interpret operating leases the same as traditional debt.

8. To determine return on capital, free cash flow, and leverage consistently, make the following adjustments on the balance sheet: *Add back securitized receivables to the balance sheet* and *make a corresponding increase to short-term debt*. The fees paid for securitizing receivables should be *treated as interest.*

9. Excess pension assets should be treated as *nonoperating*, and unfunded pension liabilities should be treated as *a debt equivalent*. With respect to taxes, valuations should be done *on an after-tax basis*.

10. The amortized prior-year service cost and the amortization of loss are zero.

$$\text{Net periodic cost} = \text{pension service cost} + \text{pension interest cost} - \text{expected return on plan assets}$$
$$\$350 = \$150 + \$700 - \$500$$

Revenues	$1,000
Operating costs	(600)
Operating profits (unadjusted)	$400
Revenues	$1,000
Operating costs	(600)
Net periodic cost of pension	350
Pension service cost	(150)
Operating profits (adjusted)	$600

11. A.

Operating assets	$3,000
Operating liabilities	(1,000)
Invested capital	$2,000
Book value of debt	$1,500
Book value of equity	500
	$2,000

B.

$$\begin{aligned} \text{WACC}_{\text{unadjusted}} &= 8.625\% \\ &= [900/(1{,}500 + 900)] \times 13\% \\ &\quad + [1{,}500/(1{,}500 + 900)] \times 6\% \end{aligned}$$

C.

Operating assets	$3,000
Leases	2,000
Adj. operating assets	$5,000
Operating liabilities	(1,000)
Adj. invested capital	$4,000
Book value of debt	$1,500
Leases	2,000
Book value of equity	500
	$4,000

D.
$$\begin{aligned}\text{WACC}_{\text{adjusted}} &= 6.977\% \\ &= [900/(1,500 + 900 + 2,000)] \times 13\% \\ &\quad + [1,500/(1,500 + 900 + 2,000)] \times 6\% \\ &\quad + [2,000/(1,500 + 900 + 2,000)] \times 5\%\end{aligned}$$

21

Alternative Measures of Return on Capital

1. C
2. For all but the *information technology (IT)* sector, the difference between CFROI and ROIC estimates is *relatively small.*
3. In both the case when R&D is expensed and when it is capitalized, the general pattern of ROIC is the same over time. In both cases, in the early years ROIC will rise dramatically. Initially, ROIC with capitalized R&D will be higher than that with expensed R&D. Very soon, however, ROIC with expensed R&D will become higher. Soon after that, both ROICs stabilize, with expensed R&D typically remaining higher. It can be the case, however, that ROIC with capitalized R&D may start to decline while the ROIC with expensed R&D continues to rise.
4. More value is created from additional growth when ROIC is relatively higher, and more value is created from additional ROIC when growth is relatively higher. Therefore, not knowing the true ROIC can lead to an incorrect focus. Managers may pursue growth strategies, when they should be focusing on increasing ROIC. Furthermore, growth can destroy value if ROIC is below the cost of capital. Therefore, not knowing the true ROIC can actually lead to managers engaging in strategies that destroy value.
5. When increasing the length of life from 6 years to 12 years, the ROIC falls by less than one-fifth in both the case of a constant 5 percent and the case of a constant 15 percent R&D expense as a proportion of revenues. Thus, doubling the length of life has a relatively small effect on the ROIC. In fact, increasing the estimated life beyond an estimated two-year life has a rapidly diminishing effect on ROIC.

6. The pattern of decline in ROIC from extending the estimated life is about the same, proportionally, for the assumed 5 percent of revenues expense rate, and the 15 percent of revenues expense rate. In both cases, ROIC declines at a decreasing rate from each two-year increase in the estimated life. The proportional decline when going from two years to four years is 18.5 percent and 26.6 percent for the 5 percent case and the 15 percent case, respectively. The proportional decline when going from 10 years to 12 years is 4.3 percent and 3.3 percent for the 5 percent case and the 15 percent case, respectively.

   The implications are that beyond a certain point, increasing the estimated life has a relatively small effect on ROIC. The most important point is that an analyst should capitalize R&D, but details such as the estimated life may have only a marginal effect.

7.

	Year			
	1	2	3	4
Sales	1,000	1,100	1,210	1,331
Production expenses	(500)	(550)	(605)	(665.5)
R&D	(50)	(55)	(60.5)	(66.55)
Depreciation	(200)	(200)	(202)	(206)
Operating income	250	295	342.5	392.95
Beg. of year capital	2,000	2,000	2,020	2,060
Investment	(200)	(220)	(242)	(266.2)
ROIC	12.50%	14.75%	16.96%	19.08%
Adj. beg. of year capital	2,180	2,212	2,265.8	2,341.72
Adj. depreciation	(218)	(221.2)	(226.58)	(234.17)
Adj. operating income	282	328.8	378.42	431.328
Adj. ROIC	12.94%	14.86%	16.70%	18.42%

8. When comparing the performance of businesses with very different capital intensity and size, using *economic profit (EP) over revenues* provides the best insights into performance and value creation.

22

Inflation

1. A. Real
   B. Real
   C. Nominal
   D. Real
   E. Nominal
   F. Real
   G. Real
2. A. Assets and liabilities are recorded at historical cost and not revalued to current levels of currency units.
   B. Nominal year-to-year comparisons and ratio analysis (e.g., ROIC and PP&E/revenue) become meaningless.
   C. Continuing-value cash flows require growth and expected returns to reflect highly variable economic conditions.
3. A. Ensure that the WACC estimates in real terms ($WACC^R$) and nominal terms ($WACC^N$) are defined consistently with the inflation assumptions in each year.
   B. The value driver formula as presented in Chapter 12 should be adjusted when estimating continuing value in real terms. The returns on capital in real-terms projections overestimate the economic returns in the case of positive net working capital. The free cash flow in real terms differs from the cash flow implied by the value driver formula by an amount equal to the annual monetary loss on net working capital.
   C. When using the continuing-value formulas, make sure the explicit forecast period is long enough for the model to reach a steady state with constant growth rates of free cash flow.

4. A. Real forecasts make it impossible to calculate taxes correctly and easily lead to errors in calculating working capital changes; companies grow in real terms when operating efficiencies improve.
   B. The main downside of using nominal cash flows is that future capital expenditures are difficult to project because the typically stable relationship between revenues and fixed assets does not hold under high inflation. As a result, depreciation charges also are difficult to project.
5. A. Forecast operating performance in real terms.
   B. Build financial statements in nominal terms.
   C. Build financial statements in real terms.
   D. Forecast the future free cash flows in real and nominal terms from the projected income statements and balance sheets.
   E. Estimate DCF value in real and nominal terms.
6. $$FCF^R = \left[\left(1 - \frac{4\%}{10\%}\right) \times \$2{,}000\right] - \left[\$1{,}000 \times \left(1 - \frac{200}{300}\right)\right] = \$866.67$$
7. The first step is to find the real values, NWC^R_{t-1} and the increase in NWC^R_t.

   $NWC^R_{t-1} = 100/2 = 50$
   $NWC^R_t = 200/2.5 = 80$
   Increase in $NWC^R = 80 - 50 = 30$
   Investment in NWC^R_t = Increase in $NWC^R + NWC^R_{t-1}(1 - IX_{t-1}/IX_t)$
   Investment in $NWC^R_t = 30 + 50 \times (1 - 2/2.5) = 40$

8. $WACC^R = (1 + WACC^N)/(1 + i) - 1$
   $G^R = g^R - [(NWC^R/IC^R) \times (i/(1 + i))]$
   $CV^R = (1 - G^R/ROIC^R) \times (NOPLAT^R)/(WACC^R - g^R)$
   $WACC^R = (1 + 0.21)/(1 + 0.1) - 1 = 0.10$
   $G^R = .04 - [(1{,}500/10{,}000) \times (0.1)/(1.1)] = 0.02636 = 2.636\%$
   $CV^R = (1 - 0.02636/.06) \times (3{,}000)/(.10 - .04) = 28{,}033.33$

9.

	Year 1	Year 2
Sales	2,000	2,320
EBITDA	600	640
Depreciation	400	400
EBITA	200	240
Gross property, plant, and equipment	4,000	4,080
Cumulative depreciation	2,500	2,500
Invested capital	1,500	1,580
EBITDA	600	640
Capital expenditures	400	480
Free cash flow (FCF)	200	160
EBITA growth	–	20%
EBITA/sales	10%	10.34%
Return on invested capital	13.33%	16.00%
FCF growth	–	–20%

23

Cross-Border Valuation

1. A. Temporal method.
   B. Current method.
   C. Current method.
   D. Inflation-adjusted current method.
2. Under the forward-rate method, the analyst will convert each of the projected cash flows in the foreign currency into the domestic currency using the forward rate for that horizon. It is more complex because it involves a conversion for each cash flow. In addition to the extra calculations, forward rates may not exist beyond a certain horizon. This means the analyst must estimate synthetic forward exchange rates using interest rate parity theory. According to that theory, changes in foreign exchange rates follow the ratio of expected inflation rates between two currencies.
3. A. Inflation assumptions underlying cash flow projections in a specific currency need to be consistent with inflation assumptions underlying interest rates in that currency.
   B. Forward exchange rates between two currencies need to be consistent with inflation and interest rate differences between those currencies.
   C. Cash flow projections need to be converted from one currency into another at forward exchange rates.
4. The stock market indexes in many countries do not represent large, diversified portfolios. In most European countries, only 25 to 40 companies account for the majority of their stock markets' total capitalization, and they are often from a limited range of industries. The table in Exhibit 23.4 from the text shows that the industries in the index can explain between 19 and 62 percent, with an average of 49 percent, of the returns of each of the various indexes.

5. **Monetary Data for Computing the Present Value of a Norwegian Subsidiary of an American Corporation**

	Year 1	Year 2	Year 3	Year 4	Year 5	Year 6
Foreign currency (Norwegian kroner—NOK)						
Cash flows						
Nominal cash flow	300	320	340	365	395	440
Real cash flow	297.03	313.73	333.33	354.37	383.50	427.18
Inflation (percent)	1.00	2.00	2.00	3.00	3.00	3.00
Interest rates (percent)						
Real interest rate	2.00	2.00	2.00	2.00	2.00	2.00
Nominal forward interest rate	3.02	4.04	4.04	5.06	5.06	5.06
Nominal interest yield	3.02	3.53	3.70	4.04	4.24	4.38
Spot exchange rate NOK/USD	5					
Forward exchange rate	4.90	4.86	4.76	4.72	4.62	4.54
Domestic currency (U.S. dollars—USD)						
Interest rates						
Nominal interest yield	5.06	5.06	5.40	5.57	5.88	6.09
Nominal forward interest rate	5.06	5.06	6.09	6.09	7.12	7.12
Real interest rate	3.00	3.00	3.00	3.00	3.00	3.00
Inflation (percent)	2.00	2.00	3.00	3.00	4.00	4.00
Cash flows						
Real cash flow	59.99	64.61	69.33	75.15	82.13	93.28
Nominal cash flow	61.19	65.91	71.41	77.41	85.41	97.01

6. **Discounted Cash Flows and Present Value of Subsidiary**

NOK discount rate	0.971	0.933	0.897	0.854	0.812	0.773
PV of NOK cash flows	291.21	298.56	304.90	311.55	320.92	340.27
Sum of PV of NOK cash flows	1,867.4					
PV of NOK CFs × Spot rate	373.48					
USD discount rate	0.952	0.906	0.854	0.805	0.751	0.702
PV of NOK CFs × Forward rates	58.24	59.71	60.98	62.31	64.18	68.05
Sum of PV of USD cash flows	373.48					

24

Case Study: Heineken

1. A.

	Historic	Forecast		
Conservative	**2014**	**2015**	**2016**	**2017**
Working capital	193.000	231.525	277.83	333.396
Net fixed assets	246.000	296.352	355.622	426.747
Invested capital	439.000	527.877	633.452	760.143
Net investment		88.877	105.575	126.690
Debt	314.000	343.12	411.744	494.093
Equity	125.000	184.757	221.708	266.050
Sales growth		**20.00%**	**20.00%**	**20.00%**
Net sales	**1,029.00**	1,234.80	1,481.76	1,778.11
Operating expense		(926.1)	(1,111.32)	(1,333.58)
SG&A		(229.673)	(275.607)	(330.729)
Depreciation		(31.20)	(37.44)	(44.928)
Operating income		47.828	57.393	68.871
Taxes on EBIT		(19.131)	(22.957)	(27.548)
Change in deferred tax		2.396	2.875	3.450
NOPLAT		31.092	37.310	44.772
ROIC		7.08%	7.07%	7.07%
Debt/invested capital		**65.00%**	**65.00%**	**65.00%**
Equity/invested capital		35.00%	35.00%	35.00%
Tax rate	−21.62%	**40.00%**	**40.00%**	**40.00%**

Conservative	Historic 2014	Forecast 2015	2016	2017
Interest rate	5.10%	**6.00%**	**7.00%**	**7.00%**
Growth (investment/capital)		20.25%	20.00%	20.00%
Investment rate (growth/ROIC)		285.87%	282.99%	282.99%
EBIT/sales		3.873%	3.873%	3.873%
Sales/invested capital		2.813	2.807	2.807
Working capital/sales	18.756%	**18.750%**	**18.750%**	**18.750%**
NFA/sales	23.907%	24.000%	24.000%	24.000%
Operating expense/sales	74.344%	**75.000%**	**75.000%**	**75.000%**
SG&A/sales	18.562%	**18.600%**	**18.600%**	**18.600%**
Depreciation/sales	2.527%	**2.527%**	**2.527%**	**2.527%**
Change in deferred tax/sales	0.194%	**0.194%**	**0.194%**	**0.194%**
Free cash flow		(57.787)	(68.268)	(81.921)

B.

Aggressive	Historic 2014	Forecast 2015	2016	2017
Working capital	193.000	270.113	378.158	529.421
Net fixed assets	246.000	345.744	484.042	677.658
Invested capital	439.000	615.857	862.199	1,207.079
Net investment		176.857	246.343	344.880
Debt	314.000	400.307	560.429	784.601
Equity	125.000	215.550	301.770	422.478
Sales growth		**40.00%**	**40.00%**	**40.00%**
Net sales	**1,029.000**	1,440.600	2,016.840	2,823.576
Operating expense		(1,066.04)	(1,472.29)	(2,061.21)
SG&A		(230.496)	(322.694)	(451.772)
Depreciation		(36.015)	(50.421)	(70.589)
Operating income		108.045	171.431	240.004
Taxes on EBIT		(43.218)	(68.573)	(96.002)
Change in deferred tax		2.795	3.913	5.478

	Historic	**Forecast**		
Aggressive	**2014**	**2015**	**2016**	**2017**
NOPLAT		67.622	106.772	149.48
ROIC		15.40%	17.34%	17.34%
Debt/invested capital		**65.00%**	**65.00%**	**65.00%**
Equity/invested capital		35.00%	35.00%	35.00%
Tax rate	–21.62%	**40.00%**	**40.00%**	**40.00%**
Interest rate	5.10%	**6.00%**	**7.00%**	**7.00%**
Growth (investment/capital)		40.29%	40.00%	40.00%
Investment rate (growth/ROIC)		261.54%	230.72%	230.72%
EBIT/sales		7.500%	8.500%	8.500%
Sales/invested capital		3.282	3.275	3.275
Working capital/sales	18.756%	**18.750%**	**18.750%**	**18.750%**
NFA/sales	23.907%	24.000%	24.000%	24.000%
Operating expense/sales	74.344%	**74.000%**	**73.000%**	**73.000%**
SG&A/sales	18.562%	**16.000%**	**16.000%**	**16.000%**
Depreciation/sales	2.527%	**2.500%**	**2.500%**	**2.500%**
Change in deferred tax/sales	0.194%	**0.194%**	**0.194%**	**0.194%**
Free cash flow		(109.235)	(139.571)	(195.400)

2. A.

$ million	**Today**	**Year 1**	**Year 2**	**Year 3 (for CV)**
Revenues	300.0	318.0	337.1	357.3
Operating costs	(270.0)	(286.2)	(303.4)	(321.6)
Operating margin	30.0	31.8	33.7	35.7
Operating taxes	–	(8.0)	(8.4)	(8.9)
NOPLAT	–	23.9	25.3	26.8
Net investment	–	(9.5)	(10.1)	**CV**
Free cash flow	–	14.3	15.2	402.0

$ million	**Today**	**Year 1**	**Year 2**	**Year 3 (for CV)**
Discounted cash flow				
Discount factor	–	0.91	0.83	0.83
Discounted cash flow	–	13.0	12.5	332.2
	$ million	**% of total**		
Discounted cash flow	25.5	7.1%		
Present value of CV	332.2	92.9%		
Value of operations	357.8	100.0%		

B.

$ million	**Today**	**Year 1**	**Year 2**	**Year 3**	**Year 4**	**Year 5**	**Year 6 (for CV)**
Revenues	300.0	318.0	337.1	357.3	378.7	401.5	425.6
Operating costs	(270.0)	(286.2)	(303.4)	(321.6)	(340.9)	(361.3)	(383.0)
Operating margin	30.0	31.8	33.7	35.7	37.9	40.1	42.6
Operating taxes	–	(8.0)	(8.4)	(8.9)	(9.5)	(10.0)	(10.6)
NOPLAT	–	23.9	25.3	26.8	28.4	30.1	31.9
Net investment	–	(9.5)	(10.1)	(10.7)	(11.4)	(12.0)	**CV**
Free cash flow	–	14.3	15.2	16.1	17.0	18.1	478.8
Discounted cash flow							
Discount factor	–	0.91	0.83	0.75	0.68	0.62	0.62
Discounted cash flow	–	13.0	12.5	12.1	11.6	11.2	297.3
Value of operations							
	$ million	**% of total**					
Discounted cash flow	60.5	16.9%					

	$ million	% of total
Present value of CV	297.3	83.1%
Value of operations	357.8	100.0%

C. Value is the same for each horizon. This is because the calculation for free cash flow, and its associated present value, is consistent for the two cases. All that has happened in the valuation is a different split on the same value. Both add up to the same amount, 357.8, because both are effectively using the same cash flow streams. The continuing value in part (A) represents about 93 percent of the overall operating value, while it represented only 83 percent of overall operating value in part (B). This is due to the earlier calculation of continuing value (in year 2 versus in year 5).

3.

$ million	**Today**	**Year 1**	**Year 2**	**Year 3**	**Year 4**	**Year 5**	**Year 6 (for CV)**
Revenues	300.0	318.0	337.1	357.3	378.7	401.5	425.6
Operating costs	(270.0)	(286.2)	(303.4)	(321.6)	(340.9)	(361.3)	(383.0)
Operating margin	30.0	31.8	33.7	35.7	37.9	40.1	42.6
Operating taxes	(7.5)	(8.0)	(8.4)	(8.9)	(9.5)	(10.0)	(10.6)
NOPLAT	22.5	23.9	25.3	26.8	28.4	30.1	31.9
Invested capital$_{t-1}$	–	159.0	168.5	178.7	189.4	200.7	212.8
*Cost of capital	–	10.0%	10.0%	10.0%	10.0%	10.0%	10.0%
Capital charge	–	15.9	16.9	17.9	18.9	20.1	21.3
Economic profit	–	8.0	8.4	8.9	9.5	10.0	10.6
Discounted economic profit							
Economic profit	–	8.0	8.4	8.9	9.5	10.0	266.0

$ million	Today	Year 1	Year 2	Year 3	Year 4	Year 5	Year 6 (for CV)
Discount factor	–	0.91	0.83	0.75	0.68	0.62	0.62
Discounted economic profit	–	7.2	7.0	6.7	6.5	6.2	165.1
Value of operations	**$ million**	**% of total**					
Invested capital	159.0	44.4%					
PV (economic profit)	33.6	9.4%					
PV (continuing value)	165.1	46.2%					
Value of operations	357.8	100.0%					

25

Corporate Portfolio Strategy

1. A. *Unique links with other businesses* include distribution lines, access to research and development, and manufacturing advantages.
   B. *Distinctive skills* include means of advertising and managing certain types of businesses.
   C. *Better governance* leads to more fruitful interaction between owners and managers.
   D. *Better insight and foresight* lead to following trends in the early years to benefit from the potential growth and recognizing budding needs in companies and consumers.
   E. *Influence on critical stakeholders* is usually more important in emerging markets, and it refers to having access to key individuals who are in government or who can influence markets when the markets are not efficient.
2. i. D and possibly A and C
   ii. C
   iii. D and possibly A and C
   iv. A and possibly D
   v. B
   vi. C
   vii. A
3. i. D
   ii. F
   iii. A

iv. E
v. B

C does not belong on the list.

4. A. Ennerall: Conglom offered capital and links with other businesses. It may have offered manufacturing advantages.
   Corwin Company: Conglom offered managerial skills, a distribution network, and marketing and sales synergies.
   B. Conglom should divest Ennerall. Conglom is probably not in a good position to help Ennerall develop new products. Conglom helped boost sales via its distribution network in drugstores, but now those advantages are over. Ennerall's managers are making large investments, which may not pay off.

26

Performance Management

1. C
2. D
3. C
4. D
5. C
6. Sustain or improve it.
7. A key issue concerning accurately assessing a company's recent strong growth is to determine whether it came at the expense of long-term growth.
8. Key value drivers should allow management to articulate how the organization's strategy creates value.
9. Diagnostics of organizational health typically measure:
   A. The skills and capabilities of the company.
   B. Its ability to retain its employees and keep them satisfied.
   C. Its culture and values.
   D. The depth of management talent.
10. A. Medium-term
    B. Short-term
    C. Medium-term
    D. Long-term
    E. Short-term
    F. Short-term
    G. Medium-term
11. A range of targets is a better system, in which there is a base target and a stretch target. The base target is set by top management and is based

on prior-year performance and the competitive environment. It is one that managers should meet under any circumstances, and not meeting this target might mean the managers would lose their jobs. The stretch target is an aspiration set by the managers responsible for delivering the target, and there should be a reward for achieving it but no penalty for not achieving it.

27

Mergers and Acquisitions

1. B
2. D
3. A
4. D
5. C
6. A
7. Three market conditions that have led to an increase in acquisitions:
   A. High stock prices.
   B. Low interest rates.
   C. A recent large acquisition in the industry.
8. A. Archetypical
   B. Archetypical
   C. Difficult
   D. Archetypical
   E. Difficult
   F. Archetypical
   G. Difficult
   H. Difficult
   I. Archetypical
9. In the case of borrowing cash for the acquisition, EPS will probably go up because the after-tax cost of debt might be low relative to the return on assets of the acquisition. The cash acquisition can destroy value for the acquiring shareholders, however, if the increase in leverage increases risk, and that increase is relatively high compared to the revenue increase from the target.

10. Many managers focus on the accretion and dilution of earnings from the acquisition rather than the value it could create. This is why many managers often choose cash for the acquisition. However, stock markets do not pay attention to the effects of an acquisition on accounting numbers.

11.

Function	Examples
1. Research and development	i. Stopping redundant projects. ii. Elimination of overlap in research personnel. iii. Development of new products through transferred technology.
2. Procurement	i. Pooled purchasing. ii. Standardizing products.
3. Manufacturing	i. Elimination of overcapacity. ii. Transferring best operating practices.
4. Sales and marketing	i. Cross-selling products. ii. Use of common channels. iii. Transferring best practices. iv. Lowering combined marketing budget.
5. Distribution	i. Consolidated warehouses. ii. Consolidated transportation routes.
6. Administration	i. Economies of scale. ii. Consolidation of strategy and leadership functions.

12. The value of the new firm will be \$102 billion, so the acquiring firm's shareholders get a 2 percent return: $0.02 = (102 - 100)/100$, but the target firm's shareholders reap a return of 33 percent: $0.33 = (8 - 6)/6$.

28

Divestitures

1. True
2. False
3. True
4. True
5. True
6. False
7. True
8. True
9. False
10. A
11. A
12. B
13. B
14. C
15.

Type of divestiture	Public or private?	Definition (letter from list)
Trade sale	Private	D
Spin-off	Public	C
Split-off	Public	G
Carve-out	Public	B
IPO	Public	F
Joint venture	Private	A

E does not belong on the list.

29

Capital Structure, Dividends, and Share Repurchases

1. A. Higher
   B. Higher
   C. Lower
   D. Higher
   E. Higher
   F. Lower
   G. Lower
   H. Higher
2. A. Internal funds
   B. Debt
   C. Equity
   The evidence does not support this ordering of choices. According to the pecking-order theory, mature, profitable firms will have lower leverage; however, large firms generating large cash flows are usually the most highly leveraged.
3. BBB (highest), A, BB, AA (lowest).
4. BBB (highest), BB, A, AA (lowest).
5. C, A, then B.
6. The market-based ratings approach uses option theory to assess the market's evaluation of the equity as a claim on the assets of the firm after paying the strike price, which is the value of the debt. It may be superior because it uses the collective intelligence of market

participants rather than the analytical tools of a rating agency. Also, rating agencies may be slow in making ratings changes, and the market-based approach can make an assessment based on day-to-day changes in the fundamentals of the firm.

7. A. +
   B. +
   C. –
   D. +
   E. +
   F. –
   G. –(Generally negative but can be positive for a firm in distress.)
   H. +
8. Conditions that justify use of derivatives to hedge risk:
   A. The risks are clearly defined.
   B. The derivatives are reasonably priced.
   C. The total risk exposures are large enough so that they could harm the firm's health.
9. A. Convertible debt makes sense when investors or lenders differ from managers in their assessment of the company's credit risk. When the discrepancy is great, it may become difficult to achieve agreement on the terms of credit.
   B. High-growth companies tend to use more convertible debt because convertible debt is less sensitive to differences in credit risk assessment and can facilitate agreement on debt terms. Such differences in assessments are more likely for a high-growth company.
10. The enterprise value initially increases as leverage increases due to:
    A. Tax savings.
    B. Reduction in overinvestment.
    The enterprise value decreases as leverage increases beyond a given point due to:
    A. The cost of business erosion.
    B. Investor conflicts.
11. Although academics argue that every corporation has an optimal capital structure, most surveys among financial executives show that executives put more emphasis on preserving financial flexibility than on minimizing the cost of capital. Empirical analyses have demonstrated that companies actively manage their capital structures and stay within certain leverage boundaries. Companies are much more likely to issue equity when they are overleveraged relative to this target, and much

less likely when they are underleveraged. Companies typically make adjustments toward a target capital structure with one or two years' delay, rather than immediately, since that would become impractical and costly due to share price volatility and transaction costs. This is also the pattern if companies were to target interest coverage: Share prices are ultimately driven by future operating earnings and cash flows. If share prices rise and remain there, earnings and cash flows eventually will rise, and that is probably when companies start to increase leverage.

30

Investor Communications

1. A
2. D
3. C
4. A. True
   B. True
   C. False
   D. False
   E. True
5. A. True
   B. True
   C. False
   D. True
   E. False
6. A. A systematic approach helps executives communicate with investors more effectively and efficiently.
   B. The objective of investor relations should be the alignment of share price and intrinsic value. It should not focus on trying to maximize the share price. A systematic approach can help align the market price of a company's shares with the company's intrinsic value.
7. A. Align a company's share price with management's perspective on the intrinsic value of the company.
   B. Develop support from a group of sophisticated intrinsic investors who thoroughly understand the company's strategies, strengths, and weaknesses.
   C. Gain intelligence about your customers, competitors, and suppliers.

8. A. *Intrinsic investors* take positions only after undertaking thorough review of a firm's ability to create long-term value. These investors typically hold relatively fewer stocks, and their portfolio turnover is relatively low.

   B. *Traders* seek profits by betting on short-term movements in share prices, typically based on announcements about the company or technical factors, like the momentum of the company's share price.

   C. *Mechanical investors* make decisions based on strict criteria or rules. This investor class is comprised of index funds, quants, and closet indexers. These investors hold a large number of stocks.

9. Knowing the different types of investors allows investor relations executives to gain insights into how the market might react to important events and strategic actions. Additionally, segmentation allows for focusing investor communication efforts on intrinsic investors, who tend to drive long-term stock value.

10. In corporate investor communications, transparency is the free flow of publicly available information. That information should be properly and fully identified, described adequately and accurately, and properly classified. Managers should apply transparency guidelines consistently to parent and subsidiaries, domestic and foreign subsidiaries, affiliates, and related entities over which the company has significant influence in order to prevent companies from manipulating financial information.

11. It is beneficial to supply information so the firm can be fairly valued. Both overvaluation and undervaluation can be harmful. Although the firm justifiably keeps some information to itself, supplying as much relevant information as is practically possible increases the chances that the managers can reduce possible gaps between the market value and intrinsic value

12. Managers think issuing guidance on their likely EPS in the next quarter is necessary because it leads to higher valuations, lower share price volatility, and improved liquidity. Studies have found no evidence that issuing EPS guidance accomplishes these goals. Managers might better accomplish these goals by providing investors with a broad set of operational measures such as volume targets, revenue targets, and initiatives to reduce costs.

13. At first glance, it appears that markets reward companies with higher share prices when they consistently beat the earnings consensus, as some research has found this to be true. However, this research doesn't take into account the underlying performance of companies as

measured by revenue growth and return on capital. After adjusting for performance, there is no significant effect on share price for consistently beating the consensus estimates. Companies with strong growth or ROIC had high shareholder returns regardless of whether they consistently beat the consensus.

31

Emerging Markets

1. F, A, E, C, D
2. Although the analyst would use some judgment in estimating the probabilities, there is evidence for determining a range of reasonable values, which is likely to be between 20 and 30 percent.

   The 20 percent number comes from the analysis of changes in GDP of 20 emerging economies over the past 20 years in which it was found they had experienced economic distress about once every five years (a real-terms GDP decline of more than 5 percent).

   The 30 percent number is from a study that found that government default probabilities five years into the future in emerging markets such as Argentina were around 30 percent in nondistress years.
3. A. Use the capital asset pricing model (CAPM) to estimate the cost of equity in emerging markets.

   B. Be flexible in assembling the available information piece by piece to build the cost of capital, and triangulate the results with country risk premium approaches and multiples. In general, be pragmatic because in emerging markets there are often significant information and data gaps.

   C. Be sure monetary assumptions are consistent. Ground your model in a common set of monetary assumptions to ensure that the cash flow forecasts and discount rate are consistent.

   D. Allow for changes in the cost of capital. The cost of capital in an emerging-market valuation may change based on evolving inflation expectations, changes in a company's capital structure and cost of debt, or foreseeable reforms in the tax system.

   E. Don't mix approaches. Use the cost of capital to discount the cash flows in a probability-weighted scenario approach. Do not add any risk premium, because you would then be double-counting risk. If you are discounting only future cash flows in a business-as-usual scenario, add a risk premium to the discount rate.

4. A. Real GDP growth, price inflation (including consumer prices), wages, interest rates, exchange rates, and whatever other parameters are deemed relevant (e.g., oil prices).

   B. The purpose is not so much to create the right economic forecasts, which may not even be possible because of the uncertainty. The goal should be to create one or more sets of consistent assumptions to apply to the valuation.

   C. Research has shown that purchasing power parity (PPP) does hold over the long run, even between emerging and developed economies. Thus the analysts should include in the forecasts the assumption that exchange rates ultimately do adjust for differences in inflation between the relevant countries.

5. The expected cash flow for the first year is:

$$\text{Expected first} - \text{year cash flow} = 440 = 0.8 \times 500 + 0.2 \times 200$$

Since the growth rate in both scenarios is 4 percent, the value of the firm is:

$$\text{Value} = 8,800 = 440/(0.09 - 0.04)$$

6. The risk premium that is consistent with the answer in Question 5 is the one that will give the same value of the scenario DCF using only the business-as-usual scenario. In other words, it solves the following equation:

$$8,800 = 500/(.09 + p - 0.04)$$

Manipulating this algebraically gives:

$$p = 0.00682 = 500/8,800 - 0.09 + 0.04$$

or 0.682 percent.

32

Valuing High-Growth Companies

1. A. Penetration rates.
   B. Average revenue per customer.
   C. Sustainable gross margins.
2. A. Monte Carlo simulation.
   B. Real options.
   C. Probability-weighted scenarios. This is the recommended method because it makes the critical assumptions and interactions more transparent.
3. The scenario weights should be based on a fundamental economic analysis for determining value (e.g., market size, market share, and competitor margins). Those estimates should be calibrated against the historical performance of other high-growth companies.
4. A probability-weighted scenario can highlight the economic issues driving a company's value. Using just a few scenarios makes critical assumptions and interactions more transparent than other modeling approaches. One can use scenario analysis to determine the value impact of changes in individual drivers.
5. The analyst should focus on sizing the future market of the start-up company, predicting the level of profitability, and estimating the investments necessary to achieve success. To do this, the analyst would choose a point well into the future at a time when financial performance is likely to stabilize, begin forecasting, and then work backward to link the forecast to current performance. Measures of current performance are likely to commingle investments and expenses, so when possible the analyst should capitalize hidden investments (even those expensed under traditional accounting rules). It is not advised to rely on a single long-term

forecast. The analyst should describe the market's development in terms of multiple scenarios, including total size, ease of competitive entry, and so on. When building a comprehensive scenario, the analyst should be sure all forecasts, including revenue growth, profitability margins, and required investment, are consistent with the underlying assumptions of the particular scenario. Finally, probabilistic weights should be applied to each scenario. The weights must be consistent with long-term historical evidence on corporate growth.

6.

Scenario	Intrinsic value ($ million)	Probability	Intrinsic value × Probability
Success in both domestic and international markets	2,500	0.3	750
Success in domestic market	1,500	0.5	750
Failure in domestic market	700	0.2	140
Expected intrinsic value			1,640
Shares outstanding: 20 million	Expected share price		82

7.

Scenario	Intrinsic value ($ million)	Probability	Intrinsic value × Probability
Success in both domestic and international markets	2,500	0.2	500
Success in domestic market	1,500	0.5	750
Failure in domestic market	700	0.3	210
Expected intrinsic value			1,460
Shares outstanding: 20 million	Expected share price		73

The price changes by over 10 percent with different probabilities. Using the initial forecast as a base:

$$\text{Percent change} = (82 - 73)/82 = 10.98\%$$

Thus, changing only two of the smaller percentages can have a sizable impact on the estimated share price.

33

Cyclical Companies

1. The three potential reasons that managers tend to increase and decrease investments at the same time (i.e., exhibit herd behavior) are:
   A. Cash is generally more available when prices are high.
   B. It is easier to get approval from boards of directors for investments when profits are high.
   C. Executives get concerned about the possibilities of rivals growing faster than their firms.
2. A. 3
   B. 1
   C. 2
   D. 4
3. The four steps for the recommended approach for evaluating a cyclical firm are:
   A. Construct and value the normal cycle scenario using information about past cycles.
   B. Construct and value a new trend line scenario based on the recent performance of the company.
   C. Develop the economic rationale for each of the two scenarios.
   D. Assign probabilities to the scenarios and calculate their weighted values.
4. C
5. D
6. True

7. False
8. False
9. True
10. True

34

Banks

1. B
2. D
3. C
4. C
5. A
6. A. Other
   B. Trading
   C. Other
   D. Other
   E. Trading
   F. Trading
   G. Trading
7.

	1988	2013
Commission income	2	2
Interest income	1	1
Trading income	3	3
Other	4	4

Although the rankings have not changed, the relative importance of these four income sources has changed radically over the past two to three decades. Most notably, European banks have steadily shifted away from interest income toward commission and trading income.

8. A.

Interest income	$67.00
Interest expense	(15.20)
Other expenses	(30.00)
Net profit before taxes	$21.80
Taxes	(8.72)
Net income	$13.08

B.

Loan spread	$40.20
Deposit spread	15.20
Equity spread	1.60
Reserve debt	(5.20)
Expenses	(30.0)
Net profit before taxes	$21.8
Taxes	(8.72)
Net income	$13.08

C. The two approaches are equivalent. The following is a proof of this equivalence. It starts with the regular income statement equation for net income:

$$\text{NI} = (r_L \times L - r_D \times D - E) \times (1 - T)$$

where r_L and r_D are the loan and deposit rates, E is the noninterest expense, and T is the marginal tax rate.

For the spread model:

$$\text{NI} = [(r_L - r_M) \times L + (r_M - r_D) \times D + r_M \times S - r_M \times R - E] \times (1 - T)$$

where r_M = the money rate of return.

The next step is to recall the balance sheet relationship:

$$R + L = D + S$$

or

$$D + S - R - L = 0$$

where R = Cash reserve
L = Loans
D = Deposits
S = Equity

Gathering the terms in r_M in the spread model gives:

$$NI = [r_L \times L - r_D \times D + r_M \times (D + S - R - L) - E)] \times (1 - T)$$
$$NI = [r_L \times L - r_D \times D - E] \times (1 - T)$$

The result is the same as the income model from the financial statements. In constructing the spread model, banks use an assumed yield, the money rate, to benchmark the profitability of loans and deposits and debit the lack of earning ability of cash reserves at the Federal Reserve. The equality of the two methods depends on the same rate being used as a proxy for the cost of equity capital. There can be a problem when using this rate to benchmark loans and deposits and the cost of equity. Each of these items has a different risk-adjusted cost of capital, and thus a different benchmark. The money rate is not necessarily related to the equity cost of capital and can be reliably assigned only to the cash reserve account. Allocations based on the spread model must be viewed with caution since they do not represent comparisons of investments (short and long) with their risk-adjusted opportunity costs of capital.

9.

Cash flow statement forecasts	**2016**	**2017**	**2018**	**2019**	**2020**
Net income	73	77	81	85	88
(Increase) decrease in equity	–90	–90	–10	–11	–11
Other comprehensive income (loss)	–1	0	1	2	2
Cash flow to equity	–18	–13	72	76	79
				CV_{2020} =	1,087.5
Cash flow value	–18	–13	72	76	1,166.5
PV(CFE) = 879.11					

$$CV = \frac{90\left(1 - \frac{0.02}{0.10}\right)}{0.08 - 0.02} + \frac{2 - 11}{0.08} = 1,087.5$$

35

Flexibility

1. A
2. D
3. C
4. B. Since there are no losses to avoid by stopping the project, the NPV is the same with and without flexibility: NPV = \$0 = –\$10 + (0.5 × \$1/0.05) + (0.05 × \$0/0.05).
5. C. $u = e^{\sigma\sqrt{T}} = e^{0.1\sqrt{0.5}} = 1.0733$

   $$d = \frac{1}{u} = \frac{1}{1.0733} = 0.9317$$

6. A. Increase in value because: The higher interest rate increases the value of the call option.

   B. Decrease in value because: The higher interest rate decreases the present value of the cash flows.
7. A. What events are the key sources of uncertainty?

   B. What decision can management make in response to events?

   C. What payoffs are linked to these decisions?
8. To value flexibility:

   A. Estimate the standard NPV of the investment project without flexibility, using a traditional discounted cash flow model.

   B. Expand the DCF model into an event tree, mapping how the value of the project evolves over time, using unadjusted probabilities and the weighted average cost of capital.

   C. Turn the event tree into a decision tree by identifying the types of managerial flexibility that are available.

   D. Estimate the contingent NPV using a DTA or ROV approach.

9. Without the option to expand, the expected NPV is:

$$\text{NPV} = -\$500 + 0.1\left[\frac{\$400}{0.25}\right] + 0.9\left[\frac{\$50}{0.25}\right] = -\$160$$

With the option to expand, the expected NPV is:

$$\text{NPV} = -\$500 + 0.1\left[\frac{\$400}{0.25} + \frac{8\left(-\$500 + \frac{\$400}{0.25}\right)}{1.25}\right] + 0.9\left[\frac{\$50}{0.25}\right]$$

$$\text{NPV} = \$544$$

10. Standard NPV $= (0.2 \times 0.5)\left[\frac{\$4,000}{(1.20)^2}\right] - \$240 - \frac{\$100}{1.04} - \frac{\$200}{(1.04)^2}$

$$= -\$243.29$$

With flexibility, the option to proceed at the end of the research phase is:

$$\text{PV(Option)} = \text{Max}\left[\text{PV (Testing)} - \text{Invest (Testing)}, 0\right]$$

$$\text{PV(Testing)} = 0.5\left[\frac{\$4,000}{(1.20)^2} - \frac{\$200}{(1.04)^2}\right] + 0.5[\$0]$$

$$= \$1,296.43$$

The present value of the development project prior to the testing phase is:

$$\text{PV(Option)} = \text{Max}\left[\left(\$1,296.43 - \frac{\$100}{1.04}\right), 0\right]$$

$$= \$1,200.28$$

The contingent NPV for the entire project prior to the research phase is:

$$\text{Contingent NPV} = \text{Max}\,[0.2(\$1,200.28) + 0.8(\$0), 0]$$

$$= \$0.06$$

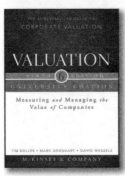

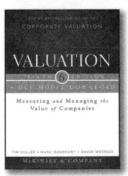